The Cadbury Committee

The Cadbury Committee
A History

Laura F. Spira and
Judy Slinn

OXFORD
UNIVERSITY PRESS

OXFORD
UNIVERSITY PRESS

Great Clarendon Street, Oxford, OX2 6DP,
United Kingdom

Oxford University press is a department of the University of Oxford.
It furthers the University's objective of excellence in research, scholarship,
and education by publishing worldwide. Oxford is a registered trade mark of
Oxford University press in the UK and in certain other countries

© Laura F. Spira and Judy Slinn 2013

The moral rights of the authors have been asserted

First Edition published in 2013

Impression: 1

Published in the United States of America by Oxford University Press
198 Madison Avenue, New York, NY 10016, United States of America

British Library Cataloguing in Publication Data
Data available

Library of Congress Control Number: 2013938417

ISBN 978–0–19–959219–7

Printed and bound in Great Britain by
CPI Group (UK) Ltd, Croydon, CR0 4YY

Foreword

First I must begin by expressing my warmest thanks and admiration to Laura Spira and Judy Slinn, the authors of this history of the Committee on the Financial Aspects of Corporate Governance. The thanks are amply due, because, without this chronicle of the manner in which the Committee approached its complex task, much of the ability to learn from its proceedings could have been lost. My admiration is fully deserved, because the authors were faced with the disappearance of the Committee's official files and had to piece their history together from such papers as I had retained, from media comment, and through interviews. Their history is based, therefore, on a considerable body of painstaking research and a high degree of commitment to establishing the Committee's place in the forward march of corporate governance, nationally and internationally.

In 1991 the Committee had already been formed when Sir Ron Dearing, on behalf of its sponsors, invited me to chair it. Although the terms of reference had not been confirmed, the broad areas of concern that the Committee had been asked to address had been identified.

The Committee had been established in the wake of the collapse of two major quoted public companies, whose audited accounts gave no indication of the true state of their financial affairs. This led to a lack of confidence in the reliability of reports and accounts and, by extension, to London as a financial centre. The Committee saw, as its immediate causes, loose accounting standards, uncertainty over the control responsibilities of directors, and competitive pressures on companies and on auditors to present results in line with published forecasts.

These concerns were broadened, soon after the Committee had begun its work, by the collapse of BCCI and of Robert Maxwell's enterprises. The failure of Maxwell's company and the fraud that accompanied it raised issues that went well beyond the remit of financial reporting and control, which had initially been the Committee's focus. Maxwell dominated an impotent board of his own selection and attempted to shore up his failing business by pillaging the company pension fund. This led the Committee unavoidably to widen its remit from the financial aspects of corporate governance to corporate governance itself, and the responsibilities and composition of boards.

The process by which the Committee arrived at its conclusions is an important aspect of its approach to its task. This is well documented by the authors. As soon as the terms of reference were agreed, they were publicized, enabling individuals and institutions to make their views on them known. This encouraged the debate and gave the Committee notice of issues on which conflicting opinions were held. From the start, the object of publishing a code of practice had been in the minds of those involved in setting up the Committee. The questions, however, were what grounds should such a code cover and how could its recommendations best be implemented?

The Committee proceeded by discussing a particular issue, such as, for example, the role of the chairman, and circulating a draft of the conclusions of its discussion for the next meeting. This would be commented on by members in writing, or at the forthcoming meeting, before they moved on to an initial discussion of the next issue on the agenda. While there were doubts at first about whether the process was too ponderous, it worked because of the quality of members of the Committee and their individual commitment. The composition of the Committee had been determined when the focus was on the responsibilities of directors for reporting and control. Its membership was later criticized for not including a current chief executive, especially when it broadened its discussions into board responsibilities as a whole.

Sir Christopher Hogg filled this gap admirably by accepting an invitation to become an adviser to the Committee. In this role, his experience and counsel were invaluable. What is important to the discussion of process is that the published Report and Code of Best Practice were the outcome of the deliberations of the Committee as a whole, with every member contributing. This willingness to work as a team made my task as chairman immensely rewarding. Our discussions were challenging but constructive, and there was a determination throughout to find common ground and to frame Code recommendations that allowed flexibility in implementation. This was important, because the Committee was conscious that current governance principles had evolved over time and that they would continue to evolve.

When the Committee took evidence on the causes of weaknesses in the way in which boards discharged their responsibilities for financial reporting and controls, it found, not unexpectedly, a wide spectrum of board effectiveness. There were enough well-regarded public companies, on whose experience the Committee could draw, for it to be able to base its recommendations on best practice. Too many directors and boards, however, were unclear about their precise responsibilities, and there was no guidance to be found in the Companies Acts on the role of boards.

The fundamental failure of board process at the time was the failure to distinguish between governance, which is the responsibility of the board, and management, which is the task of the executives, appointed and monitored by the board. The responsibilities of governance include determining a company's purpose and the strategy for achieving that purpose, setting the tone of the enterprise, and planning succession. The strict sense of accountability of boards for their stewardship is diminished if the line between governance and management is blurred. There is a temptation for boards to meddle in management, because managing is more engaging, in both senses of the word, than governing.

The Committee found the distinction between governance and management was further weakened, because the posts of chairman and of chief executive were combined in over half of the top 1,000 companies. In addition, at that time, both the role and the effectiveness of non-executive directors were under question. It was customary for chairmen to appoint non-executive directors from among the circle of those whom they knew. The weaknesses of this form of selection are obvious. Many boards at the time had too much of the flavour of a club, with collegiality taking precedence over constructive questioning and challenge. Structurally, the governance role of boards was weakened by the absence of support from appropriate committees of the board. Only just over half of the top 250 UK industrial companies even had audit committees, few had remuneration committees, and even fewer nomination committees. This meant that boards were loaded with detailed managerial work at the expense of time for governance.

The recommendations of the Code aimed to clarify the duties of directors and boards and to strengthen their governance role. They also drew the line between the respective responsibilities of directors and of auditors for the integrity of reports and accounts. The Committee's objective was to make the existing system and structure of unitary board governance more effective, not to invent a new one. Implementation of the Code was to rely on market, not statutory, regulation.

The Committee's first step in gaining support for the recommendations in its Report and Code was to issue a draft report, to encourage comment. This was to achieve two purposes. First it was to gain a mandate for the manner in which the Committee had interpreted its task. A Code of Best Practice for companies, supported by recommendations to investors, and guidance for auditors and the accountancy profession, went further than the corporate sector would have envisaged, when the Committee on the Financial Aspects of Corporate Governance was launched. Its implementation, however, depended on broad acceptance by the corporate sector. The second purpose was to test and to revise the Committee's approach in the light of informed comment. The draft drew a wide and constructive response, of which the Committee took note and which encouraged the Committee to proceed on its existing path.

The Committee saw compliance with the Code of Best Practice as being in the self-interest of companies and of investors. The basis of the Code was disclosure. Openness by companies of their systems and processes of governance was the key to informed market regulation. Agreement by the London Stock Exchange to make it a condition of listing for quoted companies to report on how far they complied with the recommendations of the Code and to give reasons for areas of non-compliance was crucial. 'Comply or explain' is perhaps the most enduring legacy of the Committee's work and one that has been widely adopted internationally.

The Committee fulfilled its remit with publication of its Report and Code in December 1992. It further published its report on compliance with the Code in May 1995, when handing over to its successor body. What was striking was how quickly and how widely companies accepted the Code's recommendations. Although the Code was directed primarily to publicly quoted companies, the Report encouraged as many other companies as possible to meet its requirements. Essentially the recommendations of the Code were not rules. They were principles or guidelines for companies to follow in ways that made sense in their particular circumstances. In terms of 'comply or explain', both were equally valid responses. Explanation carried the same weight as compliance, with the market, not the Committee, as judge of their validity. A central aspect of the Code's recommendations, being guidelines, was that they were aspirational. They did not set a floor to governance standards, as statutory rules would have done, but they formed a starting point.

While support for the Code was extremely heartening, there naturally were criticisms. Some considered that it would fetter enterprise, others that it would be ineffective. There were complaints that auditors had been let off too lightly. The most fundamental concern appeared to arise from the Report's emphasis on the importance of the role of non-executive directors and on the formation of committees of the board. They were feared by some as potentially dividing the board and thereby leading to a de facto two-tier board by the back door. This was a misunderstanding. As the Report made clear, all directors were equally responsible for the leadership of the company, and, while board committees made recommendations to the board, the decisions on those recommendations were those of the board as a whole.

I saw it as my task after publication of the Report and Code to respond to all invitations to discuss the Committee's findings and to help to overcome misunderstandings as to their purpose. I wanted to explain how the Committee had arrived at its conclusions and the reasoning that lay behind the recommendations of the Code. What was unexpected was the international interest in the Committee's work, which led to invitations to visit individual countries and to participation in corporate governance discussions with bodies such as the World Bank and the OECD. It is the wider reach of the Committee's contribution to improving board effectiveness in Britain that makes this chronicle of its work so valuable. That history would have been largely lost without the persistence and professional skill of the authors of this work, to whom we all owe a lasting debt.

Adrian Cadbury
December 2012

Acknowledgements

Our grateful thanks are due to:

Sir Adrian Cadbury whose enthusiastic encouragement made the project possible; Professor Andrew Likierman and other members of the Cadbury Committee and those closely associated with its work, who gave up their time to answer our questions and provided us with further papers; the Institute of Chartered Accountants in Scotland for assisting us in making contact with interviewees and the Scottish Accountancy Trust for Education and Research (SATER) for seedcorn funding for our early investigations; the British Academy for further funding (Small Research Grant SG100636); Professor Simon Deakin and the library staff of the Judge Business School, Cambridge, for enabling us to study the Cadbury Archive; Dr Thom Oliver and Alex Gowthorpe for invaluable research assistance; Catherine Gowthorpe and Professor Michael Page for their astute comments; and our colleagues, friends, and families for continuing support.

And remembering Professor Anthony Hopwood and Dr Paul Bircher for the conversations that originally inspired this project.

Contents

Contents

List of Abbreviations

ABI	Association of British Insurers
ACCA	Association of Chartered Certified Accountants
APB	Auditing Practices Board
ASB	Accounting Standards Board
ASC	Accounting Standards Committee
ASSC	Accounting Standards Steering Committee
ASX	Australian Stock Exchange
BCCI	Bank of Credit and Commerce International
CBI	Confederation of British Industry
CCAB	Consultative Committee of Accounting Bodies
CEO	Chief Executive Officer
CGAA	Co-ordinating Group on Audit and Accounting Issues
CIMA	Chartered Institute of Management Accountants
CISCO	City Group for Smaller Companies
DTI	Department of Trade and Industry
ECI	Equity Capital for Industry
FRAG	Financial Reporting and Auditing Group
FRC	Financial Reporting Council

List of Abbreviations

ICAEW	Institute of Chartered Accountants in England and Wales
ICAS	Institute of Chartered Accountants in Scotland
IMF	International Monetary Fund
IoD	Institute of Directors
IRC	Industrial Reorganization Corporation
ISC	Institutional Shareholders' Committee
LSE	London Stock Exchange
M&A	mergers and acquisitions
MGN	Mirror Group Newspapers
MSC	Monitoring Sub-Committee
NAPF	National Association of Pension Funds
NHS	National Health Service
OPEC	Organization of the Petroleum Exporting Countries
PIRC	Pensions Investment Research Consultants
PLC	public limited company
RSA	Royal Society for the Encouragement of Arts, Manufactures and Commerce
TUC	Trades Union Congress

A Note for the Reader

A note on the origins of the term 'corporate governance'

An account of the history of corporate governance and an examination of its many definitions is beyond the remit of this book, but it is worth paying brief attention to the history of the term. In a speech[1] to a conference on pension funds and corporate governance, hosted by Pensions Investment Research Consultants (PIRC)[2] in November 1991, Sir Adrian Cadbury said:

I'm not sure who coined the phrase 'corporate governance'. Reading through a speech by the President of the Institute of Chartered Accountants in 1934 on corporate governance themes I noticed that he did not use the term—instead he struggled with 'the machinery concerning public company administration and control'. But in other respects the speech showed little that is new.

[1] CAD 01166.

[2] PIRC is an independent research and advisory consultancy that provides services to institutional investors on corporate governance and corporate social responsibility.

Zingales (1998) asserted that 'the term corporate governance did not exist in the English language until twenty years ago'. This statement is not strictly true, although the meaning of the term has evolved. The earliest instance of its use that we have discovered is in a 1953 paper on the economic consequences of atomic attack (Cavers 1953: 33). The author, a lawyer, notes that flexibility in corporate governance would be needed with reference to US legislative arrangements, which would enable business to continue under such catastrophic circumstances. This suggests that the term may have been in use in the US in a legal context at that time.

The first extended discussion of corporate governance appears in the work, published almost a decade later, of an American management scholar, Richard Eells. The preface to his book *The Government of Corporations* begins:

During the past ten years, in various studies of the modern corporation and its role in our free society, I have repeatedly had to touch the subject of the present volume peripherally. But only within the last few years has it been possible to discuss the subject of corporate governance systematically, as I have tried to do here. (Eells 1962: p. v)

Both Ocasio and Joseph (2005) and Cheffins (2011) provided comprehensive accounts of the development of the term in the USA from the 1970s onwards. Ocasio and Joseph (2005) apply techniques of content analysis to a range of US sources published between 1972 and 2003 to map the development of the vocabulary of corporate governance. They observe:

Not only has the meaning of the term changed but it has not converged into a single meaning or concept, but instead refers to a multitude of related meanings...there is a great lack of commonality in the meaning of corporate governance. Similarly, the category of activities directly referred to as corporate governance shifted from an initial focus on business and public policy and corporate social responsibility to a concern with board organization, executives and decision making. (Ocasio and Joseph 2005: 172)

In the UK, Erturk et al. (2008) trace its use back to Tricker (1984). Tricker's influence on thinking about the topic in the UK has been significant: Adrian Cadbury has described him as 'the father of corporate governance' (Tricker 2012).

The definition established by the Cadbury Committee in its final Report has been widely adopted and is the one used in this book: 'Corporate governance is the system by which companies are directed and controlled' (Cadbury 1992).

Introduction

The Committee on the Financial Aspects of Corporate Governance—better known as the Cadbury Committee—was set up in May 1991 to address the concerns increasingly voiced at that time about how UK companies dealt with financial reporting and accountability and the wider implications of this. The Committee was sponsored by the London Stock Exchange (LSE), the Financial Reporting Council (FRC), and the accountancy profession. It produced a draft Report in May 1992 and, after further consultation, published its final Report and recommendations in December 1992. Central to these was a code of best practice (the Code) and the requirement for companies to comply with it or to explain to their shareholders why they had not done so.

The Report was by no means greeted with universal acclaim at the time, but the recommendations and the Code provided the foundation for the system of corporate governance that has developed since then in the UK and have proved very influential in corporate governance developments throughout the world.

The history of a committee that was formed for a specific purpose, took evidence, deliberated, reported, and was disbanded, may seem to be a discrete narrative, but the story of the Cadbury Committee is one part of the evolution of the concept of corporate governance, an evolution that continues to the present day. The issues that the Committee addressed are still of great concern: the complex relationships through which corporations are held to account have profound effects on all our lives. The Committee provided a framework for thinking about these issues and established a process through which such thinking could be articulated and continue to evolve. The basic principles established by the Committee were intended to underpin this evolution and to create an environment and to provide a language in which an ongoing conversation could take place among those with an interest in the economic and social contribution of companies, including policy-makers and regulators, but principally between boards of directors and company shareholders.

The regulatory framework within which companies operate may not be perfect, but it does exist and continues to evolve in a way that recognizes the importance of flexibility. The elusive notion of 'best practice' may be contested, but it offers a benchmark for the assessment of some aspects of corporate behaviour. Definitions of corporate governance may be many and varied, but they set the boundaries of the arena for debate and provide a vocabulary for discussion. These developments in the UK since the 1990s stem primarily from the activities of the small group of individuals who comprised the Cadbury Committee. This book highlights the importance of their work. Our intentions in writing this book were threefold. Firstly, to record accurately the origins of the Committee on the Financial Aspects of Corporate Governance—the Cadbury Committee. We believe that it is important to any interpretation of the Committee's work to recognize the context in which it came into being.[1] Secondly, to provide insights into the Committee process in producing the Report and Code. Despite extensive enquiries, we have been unable to locate the official records of the Committee. Our principal source has, therefore, been the papers of Sir Adrian Cadbury, now in the Cadbury Archive at the Judge Business School in Cambridge, together with interviews with several members of the Committee and others involved in its work.[2] Thirdly, to document

---

[1] Several journal articles and books on corporate governance that have been published since 2000 have erroneously asserted that the Committee was established by the UK government. Dahya et al. (2002: 461) start with the incorrect assertion that: 'The Cadbury Committee was appointed by the Conservative Government of the United Kingdom in May 1991.' This paper has been widely cited and has been reprinted in Ezzamel (2005), Van Frederikslust and Ang (2008), and Baker and Anderson (2010). Two of the authors repeated this statement in a later paper (Dahya and McConnell 2007). Other similar examples may be found in Dallas (2004: 320): 'the U.K. government initiated the development of the Cadbury Committee's *Code of Best Practice*'; Culpepper (2010: 9): 'the British Cadbury Committee was established by the Conservative government in 1990...'; Eun and Resnick (2007: 513): 'The Cadbury Committee appointed by the British government...', and Larcker and Tayan (2011: 39): 'Parliament commissioned the Cadbury Committee in the early 1990s...'.

[2] Many of the documents have been digitized and the archive can be searched at <http://www.jbs.cam.ac.uk/cadbury/>. We have cited documents from the archive using their CAD reference numbers. Further papers that have been made available to us are cited as 'Additional papers'.

the reaction to the publication of the Code and recommendations; since 1992 the principles first articulated by the Committee have become widely accepted and have formed the basis for corporate governance developments around the world. It would be easy to forget that there was initial criticism, even hostility in some quarters, and resistance to the adoption of the Code. The Committee's achievements in addressing this, and in continuing to work to establish and maintain the consensus required for the effective implementation of the Code, deserve to be recorded.

Our story begins by tracing the events that led to the Committee's establishment in 1991 and it ends with the commencement of the work of its successor, the Committee on Corporate Governance chaired by Sir Ronald Hampel in 1995. We leave it to others to document in detail subsequent developments in the UK corporate governance infrastructure and the work of the various groups, which has led the original Code through several iterations to the UK Corporate Governance Code of the early twenty-first century.

1

Setting the Scene

When the Committee on the Financial Aspects of Corporate Governance (the Cadbury Committee) was set up and began its work in 1991, the limited liability joint stock company, which was at the centre of its inquiry, had been in existence for nearly a century and a half. For a similar period of time before that, the notion of shared risk and reward had been embodied in the various forms of joint stock companies, originating in the late seventeenth century; most of them had unlimited liability.[1] Recent studies of some of those companies have suggested that in the eighteenth and early nineteenth centuries there were model 'companies of proprietors', where the shareholders (proprietors) participated actively in the management decisions and regulated their own companies (Allborn 1998; Freeman et al. 2012). Where shareholders and the companies they owned were well known to each other and in regular contact, the

---

[1] Some unincorporated companies were able to secure some of the advantages of limited liability by the application of trust law (Gower 1979).

5

problems of what we now call corporate governance were less likely to arise, although the fraudulent activities and scandals that have come to be associated with corporate life over four centuries were not entirely absent. The model of shareholder democracy, however, became unsustainable in the changing conditions of the early nineteenth century, as regional business networks became national in a changing political climate, and as joint stock companies became larger, with their investors more geographically dispersed (Freeman et al. 2012).

The emergence of the recognizably modern joint stock company took place in the middle of the nineteenth century. In Britain it was the result of three significant pieces of legislation stretching over a thirty-year period: the first of these was the repeal of the legislation known as the Bubble Act in 1825.[2] This was followed by the Joint Stock Companies Act of 1844, which allowed company formation by a simple process of registration, and, in 1855, the final piece, the Act that made limited liability easily accessible on incorporation. The legislation was consolidated in the 1862 Companies Act, providing what has been described as the then most permissive regime in Europe (Cottrell 1979: 52). However, other than a flurry of new company formation (with the concomitant speculation) in the wake of the 1862 legislation, there was no rush into incorporation until the 1880s. It has been argued that the arrival of the joint stock company with limited liability

---

[2] The Bubble Act was passed in 1720, at the time of the South Sea Company 'bubble'; new company formation and flotation had to be authorized by Act of Parliament (Ferguson 2008: 156–7).

'transformed the opportunities for financial dishonesty' to such an extent that 'discussions of business fraud filled the newspapers and journals of Victorian and Edwardian England' (Robb 1992: 3–4). Distrust of the company *per se* as well as of those who were promoting it and speculating in it remained widespread, while the partnership continued to be the most common business form in use until late in the century. As Johnson (2010: 2) concluded, 'the joint stock limited liability company...was a disputed, legally suspect and morally dubious organisational form at the beginning of Victoria's reign, yet by the 1880s it had become the primary form of business organisation in Britain'. Over the same period he notes: 'In 1801 when the London Stock Exchange was founded, it was widely viewed as a locus for morally indefensible gambling, but by the end of the nineteenth century it had become the hub of a global investment market' (Johnson 2010: 2).

This chapter charts the development of the limited liability joint stock company through the late nineteenth and twentieth centuries, in the context of the evolution of its role in business and its relationships with the market, the state, and the public to understand the wider context in which, in 1991, the Committee's appointment and deliberations took place.

The Late Nineteenth Century

A boom in company formation and speculation accompanied the 1862 legislation and was, inevitably, followed by a number of failures. The most high-profile and spectacular collapse, creating a commensurate financial panic in the City in 1866, was that of Overend, Gurney & Co., an old-established discount business, whose Quaker origins had contributed to its reputation for honesty and straight dealing. Overend Gurney had been incorporated, with a capital of £5m, less than a year before it had to close its doors. But, as was subsequently revealed when the directors were accused of, and put on trial for, having published a false prospectus, the business was already bankrupt when it was incorporated; extensive and unprofitable investments in shipping, grain trading, and railway finance, to name but a few of its many interests, accounted for its failure (Kynaston 1995: 236–40). For those who would have preferred to see limited liability more restricted, Overend Gurney's failure justified their worse fears of what might happen, and there was considerable pressure for reforming legislation. In the event, however, the Select Committee examining the Limited Liability Acts in 1867 did not recommend any substantive change (Slinn 1993: 146).

The effect of the Overend Gurney crisis has lived on: for example, in their analysis of the deregulated City in the 1980s, Plender and Wallace (1986: 230) noted that the crisis provides 'a classic illustration of the high cost to the whole economy of imprudent banking behaviour and of the contagious nature of financial panic'. The pattern of speculation and failure was repeated at regular intervals through the remaining three decades of the nineteenth and into the twentieth century, each episode leading to 'the call for legislative intervention and tougher regulation to bring wayward market operators to heel and to prevent any future market frenzy' (Johnson 2010: 3). Much the same reasons were trotted out on every occasion to oppose new legislation and greater regulation; these were, first, that business would be driven away from the City of London: 'It may be said that nearly the whole financial business of the world is now transacted within half a mile of the Bank of England, a great if not the greater part of which is carried on by means of companies incorporated under the Companies Act.'[3] A second reason was that the limited liability company was increasingly seen as playing a significant role in the creation of wealth and prosperity: the commercial freedom granted by the 1862 legislation was seen by lawyers and economists as offering opportunities for enterprise and industrial development. And, finally, fraudulent activity and dishonesty were confined to a few 'black sheep' or 'rotten apples'. Moreover, as one lawyer put it: 'It will not make anybody diligent to put it in an Act: it will not make anybody honest to put it in an Act.'[4]

There were some changes made to the Companies Acts, albeit usually small and mostly much weaker than the original proposals, as a result not only of the opposition to change in itself, but also because of an embedded

[3] Letter to the *Law Times*, 24 November 1888, from seventeen leading City law firms, opposing the Bill then in Parliament; it was not passed.
[4] Evidence to the House of Lords Select Committee on the Companies Bill 1897, paras 288–628.

hostility to allowing more state regulation. Following the failure in 1878 of the City of Glasgow Bank, for example, legislation made an audit compulsory for joint stock banks, although this was not extended to all joint stock companies until 1900 (Freeman et al. 2012). By the end of the century, however, the limited liability joint stock company was seen as the 'normal' form of business organization, replacing the partnership, which had for so long been the dominant form:

limited companies were accepted as natural, inevitable and desirable features of a healthy economy, and the only means by which Britain's receding industrial and financial greatness could be prolonged. Their origin as creations of the state was forgotten; notions of their duty to serve the public became a distant memory: their sole function was to generate a profit. Calls to subject them to greater regulation could be resisted by citing the right of private enterprise to operate free of state interference. (Taylor 2006: 223)

The First Half of the Twentieth Century

A significant feature in the corporate landscape in the first half of the twentieth century was the growth of much larger companies, frequently, although not always, created by the merger of two or more smaller companies or the acquisition of smaller companies by larger ones. Mergers and acquisitions activity (M&A) peaked, for the first time, around the turn of the century—for example, noticeably in the banking and brewing industries in the UK—and the result was much larger corporate entities. In the USA that process was already further advanced, and it was an analysis of it and its effect, published in 1932, that has become the seminal work on the separation of ownership and control. Berle and Means calculated that in the USA the assets of the 200 largest non-banking corporations totalled nearly half of all corporate wealth in the USA. This led them to conclude that the 'separation of ownership from control produces a condition where the interests of the owner and of the ultimate manager may, and often do, diverge and where many of the checks which formerly operated to limit the use of power disappear' (Berle and Means 1991: 7). This 'revolution', as they characterized it, had created new relationships between owners, managers, workers, and consumers, the implications of which were still being worked out. In Britain (and in Germany and France) a similar evolution in corporate life was taking place in the interwar years, although less quickly and less noticeably (Cheffins 2001: 88–93).[5]

Despite the growth of much larger companies in the early twentieth century in the UK, the Company Law Amendment Committee's detailed review in 1926 of the workings of the Companies Act concluded that by and large the existing legislation met the needs of the commercial community. The Committee's report noted: 'we

---

[5] There is a considerable and continuing academic dispute about how and when the separation of ownership and control took place, as well as the forces driving it. See Cheffins (2008).

realise that the system of limited liability leaves opportunities for abuse—some of these we consider to be part of the price which the community has to pay for the adoption of a system so beneficial to its trade and industry'.[6] The notion that there was a price to be paid for the benefit conferred by limited liability recurred at intervals throughout the twentieth century, even during the Cadbury Committee's deliberations, as we shall see. The Companies Act of 1929 did, however, attempt to prevent some abuses by legislating that directors must not conceal private interests that conflicted with those of the company and by introducing stricter regulation and provision for disclosure of loans and the remuneration of directors.[7]

There were, however, several significant fraud cases in the interwar years that raised questions again about accountability and whether the existing regulation was adequate. Revelations about the dubious activities of the financier Clarence Hatry in 1929,[8] quickly followed by the discovery that the Royal Mail shipping group was to all intents and purposes bankrupt, strengthened the arguments made by those seeking further reform of the law. In the case of Royal Mail, its chairman, Lord Kylsant, was found guilty, under the Larceny Act, of issuing false

---

[6] Company Law Amendment Committee, BPP 1926, vol. 9.

[7] For detailed discussion, see Edwards (1982).

[8] Richard Davenport-Hines, 'Hatry, Clarence Charles (1888–1965)', in *Oxford Dictionary of National Biography* (Oxford University Press, 2004) <http://www.oxforddnb.com/view/article/33757> (accessed 17 June 2012).

documents.[9] In another instance, in 1934, several directors were successfully prosecuted for making false statements in a prospectus in what became known as the Pepper case, and there was, at the same time, an international *cause célèbre*, the Kreuger scandal. Discussion of these and the issues they raised were the main subject for A. E. Cutforth's presidential address to the autumn meeting of the Institute of Chartered Accountants of England and Wales (ICAEW) in 1934. He began by drawing attention to the similarities of the situation in 1898, before going on to discuss the calls for company law amendment and for changes to the auditors' functions, demands that were becoming and were to remain familiar. As Cutforth noted, the effect of the scandals was 'cumulative in fostering a wide belief that there was "something rotten in the state of Denmark" and that radical alterations, either in practice, or in legislation, or in both were called for'. He went on, however, to stress the problems and difficulties likely to arise from more regulation and legislation.[10] Some half a century later, Adrian Cadbury, in an address to the Pensions Investment Research Consultants (PIRC) conference on corporate governance, resuscitated Cutforth's speech, quoting from his remarks on the 'apathy' of shareholders, and noting the 'familiar ring' of his remarks.[11]

[9] Michael S. Moss, 'Philipps, Owen Cosby, Baron Kylsant (1863–1937)', in *Oxford Dictionary of National Biography* (Oxford University Press, 2004) <http://www.oxforddnb.com/view/article/35508> (accessed 17 June 2012).

[10] CAD 03109.

[11] CAD 01166.

Old attitudes died hard, but there were, through the 1930s, arguably, some signs indicating a changing climate of opinion about corporate behaviour, risk, and its apportionment. One aspect of this was evidenced in the report of the Anderson Committee on Fixed Trusts in 1936, whose members noted: 'We found a general feeling among the business interests concerned that the healthy growth of their movement required and would be helped by reasonable regulation.'[12] With the outbreak of war, however, further changes in legislation had to wait. It was not until 1943 that the Cohen Committee began to review the formation and workings of companies and the safeguards for investors. Their recommendations resulted in new legislation in 1947, consolidated into the new Companies Act of 1948, recognizing some of the changes that had taken place in the corporate world. The public exposure of the accounting activities of the Royal Mail shipping group played a significant role in the Act's making the publication of consolidated accounts mandatory. The legislation also strengthened the protection of shareholders' interests, by provisions relating to the disclosure of aggregate remuneration of directors and share transactions.

There were also other developments in the City that reflected the change in attitudes to investor protection and the bearing of risk. In his inaugural lecture at the London School of Economics in 1950, Professor Paish argued that, these, together with the new legislation had

---

[12] BPP 1935-6, vol. 10, Cmnd 5259.

considerably increased the security with which investors might invest in public companies: he listed the significant City reforms as the greater control of applications for permission to deal in new shares exercised by the Stock Exchange, the development of reputable issuing houses, which had made the role of the company promoter obsolete, the work of the Capital Issues Committee, and the techniques and influence of the more sophisticated financial reporting. He concluded: 'While no investor can be guaranteed immunity from the inevitable risks of business, still less from the risks of national and international politics, the type of reckless and fraudulent issue which too often disgraced the first three decades of the century is now extremely rare' (Copeman 1955: 27–8). It was an over-optimistic view, hardly allowing for the ingenuity of speculators and others and a corporate world that would change radically in the second half of the twentieth century.[13]

The Long Post-War Boom: The 1960s

The austerity of the immediate post-war period finally ended in the early 1950s. Reconstruction and rebuilding helped to stimulate some growth of the economy, albeit small (Hennessy 2007: 9, 650–1). The property

---

[13] As Johnson (2010: 3) has noted, 'each set of nineteenth century regulations produced…a new array of opportunities for businessmen and financiers to develop innovative ways to operate and prosper'.

boom, which began in 1954, showed that 'property was a paradise for the tax-free profit' (Marriott 1967: 12), but the potential for further exploitation was reduced by a succession of government measures in the early 1960s. That boom, however, had played a part in the recovery of the stock markets from the mid-1950s, and that 'revived scope, at least at times, for profitable investment in industrial and commercial shares. The era also produced the new business concept of the take-over, the successful bid by one company for another to extract better value from the latter's assets' (Reid 1982: 34). There was a boom in M&A activity, some of it in key industries encouraged by government. The 'merger mania' (Davis 1970) of the 1960s involved many long-established companies in industries as diverse as car manufacture and textiles. In some of these transactions—for example, GEC's acquisition of AEI and English Electric—an organization established by the government in 1966, the Industrial Reorganization Corporation (IRC), acted as midwife. The IRC's purpose was to encourage and support the creation of large enterprises, which not only would be able to compete with American and Japanese corporations but also, in so doing, would improve Britain's flagging economic performance. The decline of British industry was a *leitmotif* of the twentieth century.

The GEC–AEI affair raised a number of questions about corporate auditing and accounting, publicly aired in the aftermath of the acquisition. In the autumn of 1967 GEC made a takeover bid for AEI. It was not welcomed by AEI, whose main defence included forecasts of a profit recovery in the second half of the year, to be continued in the following two years. It failed to impress the shareholders, who had endured years of lacklustre performance and dividends and, by early in November, GEC had secured enough acceptances of its offer for the acquisition to take place. In the spring of 1968, GEC revealed that, far from achieving the profits forecast, AEI had made losses. This, together with the publicity given in 1969 to the Pergamon–Leasco affair,[14] where forecasts again appeared to have been over-optimistic, led to a considerable public discussion, questioning, *inter alia*, the role the auditors had played in sanctioning forecasts (Jones and Marriott 1972: 331–8). Fearing imposed regulation, the accountancy profession responded swiftly to criticism by introducing a programme of accounting standard setting.[15]

Meanwhile another part of the M&A boom of the 1960s was represented by the activities of a number of young men, new to the City and eager to make money. Jim Slater and the business he was instrumental in creating, Slater Walker,[16] became the best-known exponents of this new practice of the acquisition of companies with under-valued assets. Slater Walker, described in its early days

[14] The merger of Pergamon, owned by Robert Maxwell and the US company Leasco, was aborted when Pergamon profits were less than forecast. The subsequent Department of Trade and Industry (DTI) inquiry suggested that Maxwell was not a suitable person to run a public company.

[15] This is discussed in Chapter 2.

[16] Peter Walker (1932–2010) was a Conservative politician who held office in both the Heath and Thatcher governments and was a businessman (obituary, *Independent*, 24 June 2010).

as a conglomerate, although Slater himself preferred the term 'investment bank', was, by 1969, making profits of £9m a year, 'and Slater himself was worth at least £4 million' (Davis 1970: 217). His success at the time inevitably created a crop of imitators.[17] Later, there were harsher and more critical judgements of what Slater and his ilk had done: 'in reality it was a systematic, quite shameless insider-dealing operation' (Kynaston 2002: 455). At the same time, it was noted, although not yet with alarm, that institutional share ownership[18] was increasing as a proportion of the ownership of UK equities. In 1957 it had been 18 per cent and by 1963 it had risen to nearly 26 per cent, reaching more than 30 per cent by the end of the decade (Littlewood 1998: 257, 442).

The large public companies in which the insurance companies and pension funds invested dominated the corporate sector in the 1960s. Their most significant characteristics have been described, fifty years on, by Sir Christopher Hogg, who as a young man joined Courtaulds, then one of the UK's most significant blue-chip companies, in the following terms:

If I look back to the foothills of my managerial life in the 1960s, I can now see how narrowly preoccupied I was with details of what made executive management effective. I regarded Board positions as status symbols for executives who had made it. In that era it was the Managing Directors (now called CEOs) who dominated the corporate landscape. Boards were usually very

---

[17] For a detailed account of Slater's career, see Raw (1978).
[18] Pension funds, insurance companies, unit and investment trusts.

much their appendages. The members of Boards were certainly not stupid. They were simply the prisoners of their times, as we all are.

The management of large quoted enterprises was then conducted in a rather different environment from today's, both administratively and politically. Accounting standards gave great latitude. Work forces tended to be exploited, not led, and union relationships were all too frequently adversarial. The corrupting effects of corporate power were checked only in the last resort by others; or by the CEO himself exceptionally. Non-executive directors were few and far between. An imperial culture, deeply engrained but then approaching its twilight, shaped attitudes to 'being in trade'. Money-making in the City was OK, perhaps because it was largely invisible. On the whole money-making was regarded as a disreputable motive in the leaders of business. There was a marked absence of foreign participation in management and share ownership alike.[19]

The 1970s: A Troubled Decade

Descriptions of the 1970s include not only a 'state of emergency' (Sandbrook 2011) but also 'when the lights went out'[20] to convey the impression of a decade of 'turmoil and disillusion' in the relations between businesses and the state (Boswell and Peters 1997: 1). In the wider context of international financial volatility, following the ending of the Bretton Woods agreement and the

---

[19] The Charkham lecture, delivered at the Mansion House, 14 June 2007.
[20] The title of Beckett (2009).

19

oil-price shocks, in the UK rising inflation and industrial discontent led the economy to 'the edge of the abyss' in 1976, relieved only by a loan from the International Monetary Fund (IMF) (McIntosh 2006: 265–325). Some forty years on, the 1970s is seen as a watershed:

For three decades following the war, economists, politicians, commentators and citizens all agreed that high public expenditure, administered by local or national authorities with considerable latitude to regulate economic life at many levels, was good policy…The market was kept in its place, the state accorded a central role in peoples' lives and social services given precedent over other government expenditure. (Judt 2011: 62)

The post-war consensus, which had underpinned the mixed economy, was crumbling.

At the start of the decade the collapse of Rolls-Royce (the company was placed in receivership in February 1971) shocked the City and the public. The company's difficulties had started in the 1960s, when, in order to compete in a more competitive world market and capture part of the US market, it had begun the development of the RB211 engine. In 1968 it had signed a contract for the engines with Lockheed. But it soon became clear that the contract would cost much more than originally envisaged. Despite financial help from the IRC in 1970 and promises of more financial assistance from the clearing banks and the Bank of England, the company felt it should discontinue the RB211 development programme (Capie 2010: 786–90). Receivership and public ownership (lasting until 1987) followed.

Analysing the Rolls-Royce crisis, Bowden noted not only that the company went to 'great lengths to hide from the shareholders the extent of its financial difficulties', but also that what we would now describe as its internal corporate governance mechanisms were unworkable. The composition, the roles, and the communication between the main board and divisional boards were all 'problematic'; non-executive directors 'were outnumbered and did not have full access to the information which might have alerted them to the problems the company was building up'. Pressure for managerial changes came from the banking community, but it was too little and too late, dictated only by the crisis. She concluded: 'the investigation of corporate governance under such conditions underlines the weaknesses of external and internal mechanisms of corporate governance in this country' (Bowden 2002: 61–2).

Publicly, at least, 1972 appeared to be more prosperous. There were several factors helping to make the environment 'more hospitable than before to new money enterprises' (Reid 1982: 23). These were, first, the provision in the 1967 Companies Act that allowed the creation of a new category of banking enterprises (these became known as the secondary or fringe banks) and, secondly, the relaxation of credit controls through the 1960s. Finally, the introduction by the Bank of England, in 1971, of the government-approved Competition and Credit Control plan abolished a number of further financial constraints. All these, combined in the early 1970s with the tax-cutting budgets of the Heath government, intended to stimulate greater economic growth, created a climate in the City where 'easy credit, paper empires and new-style financiers' feverishly flourished (Reader and Kynaston 1998: 146). There was in the City in the 1970s 'a formidable culture of mutual favours...There was also still an obdurate culture of secrecy and lack of accountability' (Kynaston 2002: 427).

The year 1973, however, was perhaps the corporate sector's 'annus horribilis', the worst for many a year before or since. In May there was the Lonrho scandal in the headlines. 'Tiny' Rowland was one of the UK's 'best known and most flamboyant entrepreneurs', and under his control the company, originally a mining enterprise, had added trading rights and newspapers to its activities. He had bribed African officials, defied international sanctions against Rhodesia, and systematically hidden from his own board various other activities. The boardroom battle to remove him was protracted, and even reached the House of Commons, where the Prime Minister told its members that Lonrho represented 'the unpleasant and unacceptable face of capitalism' (Sandbrook 2011: 525–6). In October 1973 the Organization of the Petroleum Exporting Countries (OPEC) raised the price of oil by 70 per cent and, two months later, in December, the secondary banking crisis erupted. Cedar Holdings, specializing in second mortgages and with considerable property interests, was on the verge of collapse and, it was feared, would take others with it were it to do so, with 'dangerous repercussions' for the entire banking system (Reid 1982: 3). Many of the new banking enterprises created in the 1960s had been guilty of reckless lending, it emerged, and disaster was averted only by the action of the Bank of England in creating what was termed the Lifeboat, funded by the banks.[21]

Even before what was seen as the largest banking emergency of the twentieth century, concerns had been developing about the state of the economy, about industrial relations and corporate performance. Behind the scenes through all this there had been discussions that generated a number of initiatives. In September 1970 an internal memorandum at the IRC noted: 'I think we all share the view that company law reform in the UK is vital—by reform one means a total re-think of the responsibilities and rights of shareholders, directors and company boards.'[22] They were not, however, optimistic about the prospect as the Conservative administration took power. And, indeed, the IRC was soon abolished. However, in 1971 a series of meetings and dinners was held to discuss the potential for a City initiative, headed by the Bank of England, which wished to 'avoid any Government action in seeking to promote greater efficiency in British industry'.[23] After a great deal of to-ing and fro-ing, two working parties emerged from this, their establishment announced in March 1972. The Bank of England's working party was to explore ways for the investing institutions to play a role in securing good management; by the

---

[21] For detail, see Reid (1982) and Capie (2010).
[22] NA, FV 44/103, M. J. Knight to C. H. Villiers.
[23] NA, FV 62/8.

autumn it had become a 'ginger group'. Subsequently it played a part in the creation of the Institutional Shareholders' Committee (ISC), the umbrella body for the insurance companies, pension funds, and unit and investment trusts (Charkham 1993).

The second working party was established by the Confederation of British Industry (CBI) as the Committee on Company Affairs, headed by Viscount Watkinson[24] and charged with 'examining the whole area of corporate responsibilities' (Watkinson 1973: 1). The reasons for this were set out in the interim report, published in January 1973, and are worth noting, given how they resonate with (and differ from) some of the purposes of the Cadbury Committee two decades later:

we have sought to take account of some of the accusations commonly levelled against private enterprise and the sort of society it creates, serves and sustains. For example, the present structure of business lends itself to an increasing, and dangerous, separation between ownership and control. That directors are not effectively supervised by those whose interests they have a duty to serve. That there is a degree of alienation of those who work in the business from those who manage it and that the lack of common purpose that this engenders corrodes industrial relations and weakens industrial efficiency. Finally that the interests of the workers are too often ignored when major changes affecting their livelihoods are being planned and that

---

[24] See Patrick Cosgrave, 'Watkinson, Harold Arthur, Viscount Watkinson (1910–1995)', in *Oxford Dictionary of National Biography* (Oxford University Press, 2004) <http://www.oxforddnb.com/view/article/60347> (accessed 17 June 2012).

in pursuit of profit the interests of third parties, whether in the character of creditors, customers or the public at large, are too often relegated to the background. (Watkinson 1973: 2)

The emphasis the Watkinson Committee gave to industrial relations matters reflected not only the growing industrial unrest, particularly evidenced in the then recent miners' strike (January–February 1972),[25] but also concerns with the EU Fifth Company Law Directive, the first draft of which was published in 1972. It contained proposals for the mandatory establishment of two-tier boards of directors, to include worker representatives (Davies 1978: 245–6). Most of the UK's senior corporate managers were vehemently opposed to this, but it was not until a later draft of the Directive, in 1983, that the proposals were dropped. In 1975 the government appointed a committee, chaired by Alan Bullock, to inquire into and report on industrial democracy. Two years later the committee issued two reports—the majority recommending worker participation on company boards, but also a minority report produced by the employer members of the committee.[26] In the event no action was taken.

The Watkinson Report went on to make a number of recommendations, including that a code of corporate

---

[25] See Sandbrook (2011: 115–30).

[26] Wilfrid Knapp, 'Bullock, Alan Louis Charles, Baron Bullock (1914–2004)', in *Oxford Dictionary of National Biography* (Oxford University Press, January 2008); online edn, October 2009 <www.oxforddnb.com/view/article/94810> (accessed 1 September 2012).

conduct should be constructed, that the chairman and chief executive positions should be held separately, and that the inclusion of non-executive directors on the board was 'highly desirable'. None of these had been wholly accepted by 1991 when the Cadbury Committee started to deliberate, but all were, as we shall see, on the agenda. However, the Watkinson Committee's most lasting legacy is to be seen in the establishment of PRO NED, the organization set up to lobby for and encourage the appointment of non-executive directors.

Non-Executive Directors

It was in the 1970s that the view that 'company boards need a leavening of high-quality non-executive directors'[27] was articulated most clearly, paving the way for the Cadbury Committee's proposals in 1991–2 to enhance their role in corporate governance. Before that, other than professional advisers (principally accountants and lawyers), non-executive directorships had most often been seen as a refuge for long-serving senior employees, retired armed services personnel, out-of-office politicians, titled members of the upper classes, and friends and relations of board members. In the second half of the twentieth century the number of practising accountants who took on non-executive directorships began to

[27] Sir David Walker, of Lord Benson (obituary, *Independent*, 13 March 1995).

decline, because of fears of conflicts of interest (Matthews et al. 1998: 204). An accountant who did take on the role for the Lucas companies in the 1950s gave his view of the role, emphasizing the need to listen:

> In some respects we were rather like a marriage guidance council; the very process of talking to an outsider helps to solve your problems…The non-executive director does have another function…to act as an independent group on matters on which our different experiences make us specially qualified to judge. (quoted in Matthews et al. 1998: 205)

Similar sentiments were voiced some years later by another experienced non-executive. Writing in 1982 in his memoir of fifty years in the City, of his time as an 'outside' director in the late 1960s and early 1970s on two company boards of the Fraser family, John Kinross said:

> I have come to feel that there is wisdom in having a sprinkling of directors who are not involved in the day-to-day management of the business. Without this, there is always a danger of the board becoming too inbred. But I think it is essential for every outside director to be available at all reasonable times, for informal discussions. The 'professional director' who only attends monthly board meetings and the Christmas office party is useless. (Kinross 1982: 201)[28]

So, some eight years after the Watkinson Report, David Walker of the Bank of England's industrial side and Sir Henry Benson (former head of Coopers & Lybrand,

---

[28] There were other voices suggesting similar actions; one of the most persistent of these was that of the MP Sir Brandon Rhys Williams.

adviser to the Governor of the Bank of England) 'were able to marshall support for the setting up of PRO NED in 1981, with the backing of the Bank, the English and Scottish banks, the Institutions, the Stock Exchange, ECI, 3i, and the Accepting Houses Committee' (Charkham 1993: 388). By his own account, Jonathan Charkham was brought in from Whitehall to run the new organization; Sir Maurice Laing was its chairman until 1984, when he was succeeded by Sir Adrian Cadbury.[29] The main purpose of PRO NED was 'missionary—to sell the virtues of having more and better non-executive directors...[and its] second task was to provide an additional source of names' (Charkham 1993: 389). As Cadbury later wrote:

The Bank of England was the prime mover in establishing PRO NED and it took the lead in the matter because of its experience in helping to rescue major companies in financial difficulties. The Bank concluded that the prime cause of such corporate disasters had been board failure. PRO NED's tasks were to persuade companies of the advantages of having competent, outside, non-executive directors on their boards and to help them to find such people. The Bank reasoned that it was better to tackle the causes of failure than to have to pick up the pieces afterwards. (Cadbury 2000: 7)

Through the 1980s PRO NED continued to recruit potential non-executives for its list, publicize its work through seminars and meetings, and commission publications.

---

[29] Laing (1918–2008), formerly head of the Laing building and construction engineering business, first president of the CBI in 1965, and a director of the Bank of England 1963–82 (*Guardian*, 25 February 2008).

The Bank of England's quarterly reports, through the decade, mapped the increasing number of non-executives on boards, indicating the proportion of boards they represented. The advantages were reiterated, although the role continued to be defined in vague terms.

The 1980s

The gradual development of the concept of corporate governance—the phrase was not as yet in common use—and recognition of its importance in the 1980s took place in the context of a period of rapid change. Across the world the integration of business, finance, and communication—the process known as globalization—accelerated, while in the UK the election, in 1979, of the Conservative administration led by Margaret Thatcher initiated a new approach to the role of government and economic policy. Starting with the abolition of exchange control in 1979, the government then embarked on the sale to the private sector of the formerly state-owned industries. In a programme lasting into the 1990s, the transport, telecommunications, steel, gas, and electricity industries passed from state to private sector ownership. While the rationale for the primary purpose of the privatization programme was the creation of competition, based on the belief that this would lead to greater efficiency, there was a secondary objective, to persuade more individuals to save and invest by becoming shareholders. Although there was a small increase in the number of individual shareholders in the short term, at the time of each privatization, in the longer term the programme did not achieve that objective. The apparently 'inexorable rise of the institutional investor' continued (Kynaston 2002: 401). In 1981 private individuals owned 28 per cent of UK equities; by 1989 the figure had slipped to just under 21 per cent. While institutional ownership rose by 2 per cent between 1981 and 1989, standing at 57.4 per cent in 1989, there was significant growth (10 per cent) in overseas ownership in that period (Littlewood 1998: 442).

In the City, too, there was change in the 1980s, most notably the changes described as 'a revolution',[30] sweeping away what had come to be seen as restrictive practices, the *bête noir* of the free market, although they had embedded the separation of functions in the financial sector. The distinction between stock jobbers and stockbrokers disappeared, as well as those between the latter and the merchant and investment banks. These changes, combined with deregulation, led to a restructuring of the financial institutions in the City as well as a radical overhaul of the systems and practices of the Stock Exchange. An immediate result of this, in 1983–4, was the acquisition by banks (retail and merchant) of securities businesses, transforming the structure of the financial sector (Plender and Wallace 1986: 112–22). Even while this new structure was being constructed, the threat of an old-style banking collapse caused a scandal. Johnson Matthey

---

[30] For detail, see Reid (1988) and Plender and Wallace (1986).

Bankers (JMB), a subsidiary of the gold refiners Johnson Matthey of Hatton Garden, was one of the five London banks dealing in gold. It had, it was revealed late in 1984, expanded its loan business very quickly, with large sums lent to a few borrowers. The Bank of England stepped in to organize a rescue, but the affair led to some critical press comment and subsequently to litigation against JMB's auditors (Reid 1988: 224–8).

However, M&A activity in the 1980s was not confined to the financial sector. In the corporate sector as a whole takeover bids increased sharply in 1984 and the value of acquisitions of quoted UK companies continued to rise in 1985 and 1986; in 1985 the value was £6,398m, in 1986 £16,550m (Littlewood 1998: 355). It was in 1986 that one of the most contentious—and later scandalous—transactions took place, the takeover bid by the brewing conglomerate Guinness for the Distillers Company. The bid was successful after a battle with the supermarket chain Argyll, which also wished to acquire Distillers. Only after Guinness had won did it gradually emerge that in a secret market support operation, encouraged by Guinness with guarantees and incentives, shares had been bought (Littlewood 1998: 354). The full story emerged in 1987–8 through a Department of Trade and Industry (DTI) investigation, and arrests and prosecutions followed.[31]

Despite this, M&A activity continued to be high, peaking in 1989, when the value of acquisitions reached

---

[31] See also Guinness (1997).

£28,372m, although in the following year it fell to less than a third of that sum (Littlewood 1998: 411). There were other M&A transactions that attracted unfavourable comment and raised questions at that time. In 1987 the investment arm of the National Westminster Bank, County NatWest, was found to have covered up a failed issue it handled for the employment agency, Blue Arrow, in its acquisition of Manpower Inc. In 1988 there was a battle between Nestlé on the one hand, and Suchard, on the other, for the old-established firm of Rowntrees; Nestlé won. In the same year British and Commonwealth Holdings plc bought Atlantic Computers, in what came to be seen as an ill-advised transaction, playing a large part in taking British and Commonwealth into collapse in 1990.

As the boom of the 1980s neared its end, concerns began to be voiced again about the relationships between the institutional investors and the management of public companies, as well as about the success and failure of companies, the very concerns that had been discussed in the 1970s and left unresolved but that would be at the centre of the Cadbury Committee's discussions. In February 1990 the National Association of Pension Funds (NAPF) published a collection of essays by industrialists covering some of the issues, most particularly 'the relationships between the management of public companies and institutional investors',[32] which was given publicity

---

[32] Among the contributors to the collection, entitled 'Creative Tension', were Lord Alexander of Weedon, Sir Francis Tombs, and, future members of the Committee, Cadbury and Charkham.

in an article in the *Financial Times*.[33] Underpinning the essays was a consensus that there needed to be some change, as recent initiatives had evidenced. The Takeover Panel, responding to concerns raised at the CBI's 1988 conference, had commissioned a working party to explore whether amendments to the Takeover Code should be made. The review concluded that there was no call for 'root and branch changes' but did recommend three specific technical rule changes, which were introduced (Alexander 1990: 6–7). A year before, a CBI/City Task Force study, charged with examining 'Investing for Britain's Future', had expressed doubts about whether 'the structure of the UK financial system could be fundamentally changed', given 'the nature of the interests at stake'. Rather than radical change of a system that had developed over such a long time, the Task Force's report focused on the need for better communications between industry and investors and on the role of non-executive directors (Alexander 1990: 6–7).

Adding to the concerns raised by the British and Commonwealth failure in 1990 there were two other high-profile collapses in 1990, both of companies that had grown very rapidly in the late 1980s through acquisitions; one was Polly Peck and the other was the Coloroll home furnishing group. The context had changed, the corporate landscape had changed, and the emphasis had changed. As the CBI would indicate in its evidence to

---

[33] Plender, 'A Rocky Boat in the City: Relations between Management and Institutional Investors', *Financial Times*, 22 February 1990.

the Cadbury Committee, 'questions about companies' accountability to their workpeople, through worker representation on the board' had largely disappeared, not least because 'there is widespread acceptance of the notion that a successful business offering a good return to its owners over the longer term will also discharge its obligations to its other stakeholders: its workpeople, customers, suppliers and the community in which it functions'. The memorandum went on to say:

The main focus of enquiry now centres on the relationship between company boards and shareholders; and the stimulus for this enquiry has two causes: the high level of takeover activity in the mid to late 1980s led to the sentiment amongst many directors and managers that institutional investors did not adopt a longer term perspective towards the businesses in which they held shares; and more recently a number of large corporate failures.[34]

By the end of 1990 the stage was set for the next scene.

---

[34] CAD 03261.

2

The Context, the Catalyst, and the Birth of the Committee

The Context

The changes in the corporate sector in the second half of the twentieth century, which we have discussed in the previous chapter, were paralleled by a considerable upheaval for the accounting profession. During the 1960s, the areas of judgement underpinning financial reporting were revealed in the process of several controversial mergers and takeovers and company failures, as noted in the previous chapter. These events prompted much criticism of the quality of financial reporting and the establishment of the Accounting Standards Steering Committee (ASSC) in 1970 is generally viewed as a response to this, although this version of events is perhaps an oversimplification of the complex influences leading to this eventual outcome. In his detailed history of the first two decades of financial reporting standards in the UK, Rutherford (2007) showed that leading members of the profession were, in the 1960s, already aware of a need to bring some logical order to the range of traditional practice that had developed over many years, but reaching agreement on a way forward among the many different interests represented by both firms and professional bodies was a challenging task. The scandals of the late 1960s, and the academic[1] and media commentary they prompted, provided a focus for change, but Rutherford observed: 'The evidence is, then, that little of the scandalous behaviour associated with the cases of AEI-GEC, Pergamon and Rolls Razor involved serious differences within, or weaknesses of, financial reporting principles or methods' (2007: 7) and concluded: 'Criticism of accounting methods was to a large extent unjustified and misdirected but ultimately produced a constructive step towards improvement in accounting practice' (2007: 21).[2]

There are parallels here with the story of the Cadbury Committee's origins some two decades later, and indeed some of the same people appear. Henry Benson, a Board

---

[1] Particularly that of Professor Edward Stamp of the University of Lancaster. See Rutherford (2007) for a detailed account of the events of the time. See Zeff (2009) for a first-hand account of the background to the development of accounting standards in an interview with Michael Renshall, the first technical director at ICAEW.

[2] Not everyone would agree. Accounting standards are now such an accepted feature of the regulatory landscape that the voices that have questioned their value have been marginalized (Baxter 1981; Myddleton 2004). Interestingly, Rutherford cites neither Baxter nor Myddleton. His account of standard setting outlines critical debates about specific standards but not the entire standardization programme.

of Trade inspector into the Rolls Razor affair, was a prime mover in the establishment of PRO NED, which clearly influenced the thinking of the Committee on the role of non-executive directors. The death of Robert Maxwell and the consequent unwinding of his business affairs, first criticized in the Pergamon–Leasco affair, also affected the Committee's work. It is thus important to site the story of the Cadbury Committee within the framework of concerns about corporate behaviour that had developed in the decades before its establishment, rather than to characterize it as simply a reaction to more recent corporate scandals. These may be more accurately viewed as catalysts, prompting action by several groups of interested parties. A close examination of the influences that led to the establishment of the Committee suggests a rather more complex link between concern about corporate reporting and the response of the accounting profession and other interested groups.

In spite of the establishment of the accounting standard-setting regime, recurring financial scandals through the 1980s, as described in Chapter 1, once again highlighted apparent deficiencies in corporate reporting and weaknesses in accounting standards so far produced. The apparent oxymoron 'creative accounting' was widely used to describe practices that ranged from the legitimate exercise of judgement, with benign intent, to manipulations designed to conceal outright fraud.[3] Sir David

---

[3] For a detailed discussion of creative accounting, see Jones (2011).

Tweedie, who chaired the Accounting Standards Board (ASB) from 1990 to 2000, described the 1980s thus:

Companies were desperate to keep showing increasing profits and the ethics of the City and the judgement and professionalism of auditors began to be called into question. Underlying many of the issues were the old questions of what is a company's asset or liability, i.e. what should be on or off balance sheet. This was the age of the Guinness scandal; structured off balance sheet vehicles; and questionable sales and securitisations. This was the era of 'the creeping crumple', the picking off of auditors by investment bankers, selling a scheme that perhaps was just within the law to a client, persuading two major auditing firms to accept it whereupon it become accepted practice and QCs would tell a third auditor that he could not qualify it as the scheme was now part of true and fair. The ASC[4] with its small staff, part-time board and the need to obtain the approval of all six UK and Irish accountancy institutes could not cope with this assault on the profession.[5]

In November 1987 Ronald Dearing[6] was asked by the Consultative Committee of Accounting Bodies (CCAB)[7]

---

[4] The Accounting Standards Committee (ASC) replaced the ASSC in 1976 and was itself replaced by the ASB in 1990: more details of the history of accounting standards can be found at <http://www.icaew.com/en/library/subject-gateways/accounting-standards/knowledge-guide-to-uk-accounting-standards> (accessed 15 December 2012).

[5] Tweedie's speech to the Institute of Chartered Accountants in Scotland (ICAS) in September 2008 <http://www.ifrs.org/Alerts/Conference/Pages/Sir-David-Tweedie-addresses-Institute-of-Chartered-Accountants-of-Scotland.aspx> (accessed 27 November 2012).

[6] Later Lord Dearing, former civil servant and chair of the Post Office 1980–7.

[7] The CCAB 'provides a forum whereby its member bodies can meet and act collectively on behalf of the accountancy profession in the UK to promote the public interest on matters within the sphere of the profession and its members' <http://www.ccab.org.uk/> (accessed 12 December 2012).

to review the accounting standard setting and enforcement regime; his report (Dearing 1988) led to the establishment of the Financial Reporting Council, initially under his chairmanship.[8] But strengthening the accounting standard setter could only partially address the loss of confidence in audit. The general perception of the role of auditors in detecting problems in financial reporting has always contrasted with their role as framed in company law: the difference was illustrated in Justice Lopes's observation in 1896 that the auditor is 'a watch-dog, but not a bloodhound'.[9] This difference has

---

[8] Rutherford (2007) gives a detailed history of the first two decades of accounting standard setting in the UK; Turley (1992) explains the developments that followed the Dearing Report.

[9] 'But in determining whether any misfeasance or breach of duty has been committed, it is essential to consider what the duties of an auditor are. They are very fully described in In re London and General Bank, to which judgment I was a party. Shortly they may be stated thus: It is the duty of an auditor to bring to bear on the work he has to perform that skill, care, and caution which a reasonably competent, careful, and cautious auditor would use. What is reasonable skill, care, and caution must depend on the particular circumstances of each case. An auditor is not bound to be a detective, or, as was said, to approach his work with suspicion or with a foregone conclusion that there is something wrong. He is a watch-dog, but not a bloodhound. He is justified in believing tried servants of the company in whom confidence is placed by the company. He is entitled to assume that they are honest, and to rely upon their representations, provided he takes reasonable care. If there is anything calculated to excite suspicion he should probe it to the bottom; but in the absence of anything of that kind he is only bound to be reasonably cautious and careful' (Justice Lopes in re Kingston Cotton Mill Company (No. 2) (1896) *Lindley L.J., Lopes L.J. and Kay L.J. (Court of Appeal)* <http://en.wikisource.org/wiki/Re_Kingston_Cotton_Mill_Company_%28No.2%29_%281896%29> (accessed 15 December 2012).

persisted and in the 1970s came to be described as 'the expectation gap'.[10]

Robert Bruce, editor of *Accountancy Age* from 1981 to 1990, subsequently described the decade thus:

The 80s was the decade when huge economic growth, combined with a post-war generation reaching its early maturity, brought immense prosperity to the accountancy profession. It also sowed the seeds for its demise in the eyes of the public. In those days, there was a 'Big Eight'[11] of accounting firms rather than the somewhat diminished 'Big Four' in place today.[12] And they were stuffed to the gills with bright, young and ambitious accountants. This was the post-war generation flexing its muscles. Senior partners were being appointed to the big firms in their mid-40s. This was seen as being excitingly youthful. The older generation, built on trying to be wise and professional, were on their way out, partly worn down by the economic disasters that had beset Britain in the two post-war decades...[13]

The rapid growth that the profession experienced also brought its problems. That most traditional of issues, competition among professional firms, came to the fore. The

[10] Teo and Cobbin (2005) offer a detailed examination of the confusion around the role of audit in the nineteenth century. They identify the first use of the expression 'expectation gap' in this context by Liggio (1974). See also Porter (1993).

[11] Arthur Andersen; Arthur Young; Coopers & Lybrand; Deloitte Haskins and Sells; Ernst and Whinney; Peat Marwick Mitchell; Price Waterhouse; Touche Ross.

[12] PwC (PricewaterhouseCoopers); Deloitte Touche Tohmatsu; Ernst & Young; KPMG.

[13] One of our interviewees commented on this cultural change in a large accountancy firm: 'as a young partner...I had to learn to be robust at challenging whereas previously I had learnt to be polite and courteous and try to agree.'

Monopolies and Mergers Commission decided that, to increase competition, the profession should be forced to lift its restrictions on advertising...It was at this point that the firms had a choice. They could stick to their independence. Or they could start trimming their independence in the face of client pressure. Increasingly they chose the latter.

It was a disaster. The audit, to use the jargon, had become commoditised. In the 70s, *Accountancy Age* used to run a regular update on the number of audit qualifications. These were seen as an indictment of less than savoury financial reporting in the corporate sector. In the 80s, the audit qualifications dried up. Finance directors had the leverage and the advantage. Audit firms increasingly did not stand firm. Finance directors could sack them and claim 'commercial reasons'. This deflected scrutiny of their financial reporting and instead made the audit firm sound as though it was to blame.[14]

As Bruce vividly described, the financial scandals of the 1980s, coupled with the 'commoditisation' of audit in the context of increasing global competition within the accountancy profession,[15] led to questions about the relationships between auditors and company boards, in particular the pressure placed on auditors characterized by Tweedie as the 'creeping crumple'. The Caparo case in 1990 exposed further misconceptions about the role of audit in terms of guaranteeing the soundness of a company and the extent of auditors' liability to those relying

---

[14] <http://www.accountancyage.com/aa/opinion/1771678/aa-1980s-riding-roughshod-audit> (accessed 7 December 2012).

[15] Koza and Lewin (1999: 642–4) provided a useful description of the challenges facing the audit industry worldwide at this time.

on published financial reports.[16] There was a growing sense among auditors that they were being blamed for financial reporting difficulties for which audit was not entirely responsible. As well as setting their own house in order, they began to call for clarification about the roles of directors and investors in corporate governance. The story of the Cadbury Committee begins in this climate of concern about how to restore confidence in financial reporting and the audit process, amid overlapping debates in various arenas about the best way to encourage corporate growth and improve corporate performance, while at the same time increasing corporate accountability with a minimum of mandatory regulation.

The Catalyst

Dinners play an important part in the life of professional bodies. These formal occasions confirm the exclusivity of

---

[16] *Caparo Industries plc v Dickman* [1990] 2 AC 605. Caparo Industries plc bought shares in poorly performing company Fidelity plc and continued to increase its shareholding until taking over the company. Caparo then sued the Fidelity auditor, alleging that the company had suffered a loss by purchasing further shares and making their takeover bid in reliance on misleading audited accounts and that the auditors owed them a duty of care to prevent that loss either as potential bidders for Fidelity or as an existing shareholder of Fidelity. After an initial hearing, which ruled that no duty of care existed, the Court of Appeal ruled that the claim was good as Caparo had been a shareholder. This was overturned by the House of Lords. The Cadbury Report included a detailed appendix dealing with Caparo and relevant issues arising from the case. See CAD 03110 for a speech by the chief executive of Caparo given in April 1991 to the ICAEW London Practitioner Board.

membership, enable members to reflect on their achievements, perhaps through the presenting of awards, and remind them of their public purpose, often articulated in speeches by the elected leadership or eminent outsiders.[17] The Institute of Chartered Accountants in Scotland (ICAS) is no exception. Each year it hosts two dinners for members, one in Scotland and one in London. The London dinner serves to remind the movers and shakers of the City of the importance of this ancient body, which predates its larger competitors in the world of the accountancy profession. The Scottish body had already been in the vanguard of thinking about improving financial reporting: its 1988 report 'Making Corporate Reports Valuable'[18] had prompted considerable discussion. Its leadership was also concerned about the body's future role, following a failed attempt to merge with the Institute of Chartered Accountants in England and Wales (ICAEW). Against the backdrop of mounting criticism of the profession's role in the financial scandals of the 1980s, the incoming president of ICAS, Ian Percy, had given careful thought to the

---

[17] The role of the dinner as a communication vehicle should not be underestimated. Cadbury met interested parties at dinners—for example, the Stock Exchange Advisory Committee (CAD 01155). Throughout the life of the Committee and beyond, he spread the message through speaking engagements, which included dinners: see, e.g., CAD 01109, a letter from Sir Denys Henderson of ICI, 2 October 1991: 'I very much enjoyed our dinner at Claridge's last night and admired the masterful way in which you introduced the fascinating topic of "The chairman's role".' And, of course, the conclusion of the Committee's formal work was marked by a dinner.

[18] 'Making Corporate Reports Valuable' <http://www.icas.org.uk/site/cms/contentviewarticle.asp?article=2340> (accessed 7 December 2012).

content of his speech, delivered at the London dinner at the Savoy on 5 November 1990. While acknowledging that audit quality might leave room for improvement, he emphasized that directors needed to take greater responsibility, urging a review of the governance of British companies. Listening to his speech were a number of influential people, including the Lord Chancellor, Lord Mackay; the Minister of Corporate Affairs, John Redwood; the Deputy Governor of the Bank of England, Pen Kent; the chairman of the London Stock Exchange, Andrew Hugh Smith; and Ron Dearing, chairman of the Financial Reporting Council. Over port and cigars, Percy was both congratulated on his speech and challenged to take action. His first thought was to organize another dinner...

On 19 December 1990, Percy sent out an invitation to a dinner to be held on 8 January 1991,[19] at Chartered Accountants' Hall, the home of ICAEW, sending out a strong message that, although the professional bodies had not been able to reach agreement on forming a British Institute, the profession was united in its concerns. Invited to the dinner were both Hugh Smith and Kent, who had been present at the ICAS dinner; Sarah Brown from the DTI; Mike Lickiss, ICAEW president; Peter Johnston, ICAS chief executive; Nigel Macdonald, also from ICAS and a partner in Ernst & Young; Chris Swinson, partner in BDO Binder Hamlyn; Geoffrey Maitland Smith, a member of the FRC; Mick Newmarch from the Prudential Group; and Adrian Cadbury, then

---

[19] CAD 03257.

chairman of PRO NED. Before the dinner Percy wrote and circulated a discussion paper that expanded on the personal views expressed in his ICAS speech. It outlined the challenge of maintaining confidence in financial reporting, emphasizing the need for a regulatory framework that enabled rather than constrained business and offered a series of recommendations to address this, setting out clearly the responsibilities of those involved. The paper prompted an extensive discussion over dinner, and those present agreed that the issues should be taken forward by the establishment of a committee, to be sponsored by the Stock Exchange, the accountancy profession, and the Financial Reporting Council.

Over the next few months, a number of parallel initiatives developed. Within the accountancy profession, ICAS set up a working party on corporate governance under the chairmanship of Nigel Macdonald;[20] the ICAEW Financial Reporting and Auditing Group (FRAG) was discussing relevant topics, and its Research Board had commissioned projects on the expectation gap and on audit committees; and the Auditing Practices Board (APB) was discussing whether the standard audit report should include comment on the respective roles of auditors and directors. The large accountancy firms were also taking a close interest: in January 1991 Brandon Gough, then chairman of Coopers & Lybrand Deloitte and a member of the FRC, wrote to Sir Peter Gregson at the DTI, enclosing a paper proposing 'a speedy but comprehensive

[20] CAD 01011; CAD 01005.

review of the broad issue of corporate governance and accountability',[21] which he copied to Lickiss, Dearing, and Hugh Smith. The paper observed that 'the concepts implicit in corporate governance, such as management controls', were not covered in existing legislation and that there was 'widespread confusion about the role of the auditor'. The paper proposed that these issues could be addressed by the establishment of a committee to report on corporate governance and accountability and to draft a code of practice and set out a list of issues that such a committee could usefully address. The Confederation of British Industry (CBI) had set up a group looking at long termism and corporate governance, and in March 1991 the Association of British Insurers (ABI) produced a discussion paper on the responsibilities of institutional investors.

There is ample evidence that the accountancy profession was a prime mover in the establishment of the Cadbury Committee, but it is clear that other groups were also thinking along similar lines and were equally concerned about protecting their interests: the membership of the Committee reflected some of these groups, although the process of appointment remains opaque. The members we have asked about this recall telephone calls from Lickiss and Dearing inviting them to serve, but it is not clear how the sponsors decided whom to invite. Although Adrian Cadbury was present at the

---

[21] CAD 01003.

dinner when the decision to establish the Committee was made, and was mooted as chairman at that point, he was not formally appointed until just before the Committee's launch in May 1991, when its membership had already been agreed. Members drawn from the accounting profession were Nigel Macdonald, vice president of ICAS; Andrew Likierman, the only academic member and also president of the Chartered Institute of Management Accountants (CIMA) during 1991–2; and Jim Butler, senior partner at KPMG. Links to the sponsoring bodies were provided by Ron Dearing, chairman of the FRC, and Andrew Hugh Smith, chairman of the London Stock Exchange and a deputy chairman of the FRC. Mark Sheldon, president of the Law Society and senior partner of the City law firm Linklaters & Paines, was also a member of the FRC. Jonathan Charkham, adviser to the Governor of the Bank of England, was included, as were members of other groups with a close interest in corporate governance issues: Hugh Collum was chairman of the Hundred Group of Finance Directors; Mike Sandland chaired the Institutional Shareholders' Committee; Ian Butler was a council member of the CBI; and Sir Dermot de Trafford chaired the Institute of Directors (IoD).

Even though the interests of some of these constituencies had been reflected in the choice of Committee members, both Cadbury and the sponsors were lobbied about the extent to which the membership represented all interested groups, and these discussions continued into the late summer of 1991. Some were politely fended off. In replying to an offer of participation from the president of the Institute of Public Relations, Cadbury observed that, in his view, the Committee, which had been formed before he became chairman, was 'already uncomfortably large'. He added: 'I imagine that the aim of those who set the committee up was to ensure that the institutions which would have to put our recommendations into effect were represented.'[22] Representation on the Committee of trade unions, the Green Party, consumers, and small investors was also called for,[23] but, while these requests were considered and received polite responses, it is clear that both the sponsors and the chair viewed any increase in size and broadening of focus as unlikely to assist in achieving the Committee's objectives.

The ongoing debate about membership centred on justifying the legitimacy of the Committee's ultimate recommendations in the eyes of those who would have to implement them, rather than ensuring a broad representation of all possible stakeholders. Expertise and individual status were considered more important. Charkham, for example, wrote to Cadbury to check his understanding before the first meeting: 'I take it that we all appear in a personal not a representation capacity. This may have especial significance if in the end some ideas emerge that not all institutions collectively could support.'[24]

---

[22] CAD 01079.

[23] CAD 01063, letter from Dearing to Cadbury reporting on meeting with Austin Mitchell MP and Prem Sikka, 17 July 1991. Tim Smith, 'Neglecting the Rights of the Smaller Investor', *Accountancy Age*, 13 June 1991.

[24] CAD 01061.

Macdonald later reflected on the process of appointment:

In a way which many would consider typical of British pragmatism, the members of the Cadbury Committee were selected so as to be representative of the range of interested groups...each of us was appointed as individuals, not as representatives or delegates of the backgrounds from which we came. (Macdonald 1997)

Committee members, however, did not all share this view: de Trafford and Butler, for example, saw themselves as the direct representatives of their institutions, the IoD and the CBI respectively.

A particular concern as to whether the sponsors had fully recognized the need for the 'corporate credibility'[25] of the Committee prompted extensive discussion about the balance of the membership. On 3 July 1991, Sir Owen Green, chairman of BTR, wrote to Hugh Smith expressing surprise that none of the members was a company chairman or senior executive and suggesting that the inclusion of 'a 50 year old chairman/MD from a middle sized corporation' would 'add some extra saleability to your end product'.[26] Green did not leave it at that. On 18 July 1991 Charkham wrote to tell Cadbury that, at a lunch the day before, he had met Green, who 'promptly bent my ear about the composition of your committee. Although he recognised in highly

---

[25] CAD 01049.
[26] CAD 01065.

complimentary terms your own experience and standing, he nevertheless felt it would be an advantage were you to have another industrialist on board.'[27] Green was a persistent critic of both process and outcome,[28] offering a continuing challenge throughout the existence of the Committee.[29]

Sheldon echoed this view in a letter to Cadbury on 19 July 1991,[30] proposing the addition of a 'tough chairman and/or chief executive of high standing—possibly even two!' Cadbury's response set out in detail his view that the Committee's existing membership already contained the necessary experience, but Sheldon promptly replied that they needed 'another strong, independent, non-financial executive...one up to his neck in the cut and thrust of competitive life'. He also expressed concerns about the age balance: 'I think we should be looking for someone in his fifties—if I may say so, Ian [Butler], Sir Dermot and yourself join me in having entered the seventh decade.' He suggested several possible people, including Christopher Hogg, chairman of Courtaulds.

The matter was discussed with the Committee's sponsors. On 14 August Hugh Smith wrote agreeing with Sheldon's proposal but pointing out that it might be difficult to find a suitable chief executive with the time to

---

[27] CAD 02251.

[28] 'Why Cadbury Leaves a Bitter Taste', *Financial Times*, 9 June 1992.

[29] See Chapter 5 for details of his critique after the publication of the Committee's Report.

[30] CAD 01049.

spare: if another chairman was considered appropriate, he too suggested Hogg as a suitable person.[31]

In September Sheldon again pressed the case in support of Hogg,[32] who, by the end of October, had been approached and had agreed to assist the Committee, but, being unable to attend the planned meetings, made his contribution through continuing discussion with Cadbury and Nigel Peace, the Committee secretary. He was described as adviser to the Committee in the final Report. Notes of a meeting on 25 October[33] reveal that Hogg saw part of the Committee's role as to 'market' good corporate governance. He believed that the current system was broadly satisfactory but highlighted the role of institutional investors, arguing that they had 'a public duty of some kind to put their minds to good governance'. He also suggested that 'perhaps some form of increased cooperation between the institutions was called for'.[34] The notes continue: 'Sir Adrian said that he wanted to gear his Committee's material so as to make it acceptable to people in Sir Christopher's position. Sir Christopher would play a most valuable role by enabling him to anticipate the intelligent reaction.' Hogg has since described his role as that of a 'canary down a coalmine, to cheep and keel over if the air got too foul'.[35]

---

[31] CAD 01057.

[32] CAD 01193.

[33] CAD 01181.

[34] A suggestion that has been repeated in the Walker Review (2009) <http://webarchive.nationalarchives.gov.uk/+/http://www.hm-treasury.gov.uk/d/walker_review_261109.pdf> (accessed 27 November 2012).

[35] Interview with authors, 20 January 2010.

The Birth of the Committee

Nigel Peace, seconded from the DTI, set about establishing the Committee's support structure. The Committee was based at Chartered Accountants Hall, the Moorgate Place headquarters of ICAEW, where Patricia Snoad ran the office,[36] and all was in place by the date of the Committee's formal launch. This took place on 30 May 1991 with a press briefing led by Cadbury,[37] accompanied by Dearing, Hugh Smith, and Lickiss representing the sponsors. At this stage the Committee was still referred to as a working party. The renaming of the working party as a committee[38] was a significant pointer to the anticipated acceptability of the Committee's recommendations and code. These would carry authority and legitimacy if they bore the imprimatur of its influential sponsors— the FRC, the Stock Exchange, and the professional accountancy bodies. Moreover, it was widely recognized that the Bank of England, with its long history of advocating better corporate governance, was giving its unofficial support to the initiative, not least by providing a room for the monthly meetings (after the first, which was held at Chartered Accountants

[36] CAD 01149. Given that efficient systems were established from the start, it is puzzling that the papers have not been found.
[37] CAD 03100.
[38] This change seems to have taken place early in July. CAD 01065 (3 July) refers to the working party, CAD 01067 (23 July) refers to the Committee. However, some of Peace's notes from June refer to it as the Committee.

Hall[39]). The involvement of the DTI, through Peace's secondment as well as its presence at the Committee's meetings in the shape of a senior adviser from its Companies Division,[40] gave a quasi-official tinge to the proceedings. These impeccable credentials gave the Committee a fair wind, but, it must be acknowledged, did not make its task, described by Cadbury as 'daunting',[41] any easier.

Cadbury's draft of his speech at the briefing[42] identified the driving forces behind the initiative as the pace of change in the business environment; the rise of institutional investors; and deregulation. Noting that the terms of reference had yet to be finalized, the following issues were flagged as major concerns and would form the basis of the working party's remit: communication links between boards, shareholders, and other stakeholders; audit committees; the responsibilities of auditors; the nature, clarity, and frequency of corporate reporting; and the responsibilities of directors for planning and for reviewing and reporting on performance. Cadbury made the intention very clear:

The aim of our enquiries will be to put forward a code of best practice which will carry weight because of the authority of the

[39] A move that might have been made to distance the Committee publicly from the accountancy profession. See CAD 01243, 1 July 1991, in which Collum observed that 'the committee would lack credibility if its report appeared to be too much driven by the accountants'. However, the secretariat remained at Chartered Accountants Hall.
[40] Sarah Brown until October 1991, then Arthur Russell until September 1994, when Brown took up the role again.
[41] CAD 01139, letter to M. Lickiss, 14 January 1992.
[42] CAD 01149.

institutions which are putting it in hand and will therefore be adopted by all forward-looking companies...What is different about this particular project is that it will aim to bring together the fruits of work and study undertaken by a number of groups and it will do so in a form which will lead to action. None of us wish to be involved in compiling more paper: we have better things to do. Our aim is to contribute to the effectiveness with which companies are run.

The criteria for judging 'best practice' were not defined, but Cadbury stated firmly: 'In a moving situation, best practice has to give the lead. Regulation may or may not follow in its wake, but it cannot make the pace.'

Press reports of this briefing focused on slightly different aspects. The *Financial Times* emphasized that the Committee would not actively seek legislative changes, quoting Dearing on the damage done by legislation.[43] The *Guardian* was more interested in directors' pay, claiming that this 'currently vexed question' would be examined as part of the review.[44] This is not mentioned in the briefing note, but the topic was much under discussion in the media at the time, and there was a general expectation that the Committee would address the issue, emphasized in a report in *The Times*, which referred to the Committee as having 'some Augean stables to clean'.[45]

[43] Simon Holberton, 'Corporate Review Set to Act: Sir Adrian Cadbury to Head Committee Set Up to Review "Corporate Governance"', *Financial Times*, 31 May 1991.

[44] Alex Brummer, 'Sir Adrian Cadbury Starts on Code of Practice for Public Companies', *Guardian*, 31 May 1991.

[45] 'Hypocrisy abounds over executives' pay issue', *The Times*, 1 June 1991.

In a short space of time a group of concerned participants had galvanized significant sponsors, who had assembled a committee selected to bring a range of perspectives to the discussion and appointed a charismatic chairman. The Committee began its work in a climate of considerable interest and high expectations.

3

'Labouring in a Vineyard'

In the period of six weeks between the public announcement of the Committee's formation and its first formal
meeting, the chairman and secretary embarked on a
period of intense activity. On the one hand, clarification
of the purpose and scope of the Committee as well as
the approach it would use was required; on the other,
of the many issues that would have to be addressed, the
most pressing were the terms of reference, the way the
Committee would work, and the timescale in which it
would carry out its task. Moreover, as we have seen, by
the spring of 1991 the rising tide of anxiety about the
shortcomings in the then system of corporate governance had led to the establishment of a number of other
working parties as well as that chaired by Cadbury. The
Committee was, therefore, working in a 'vineyard' of
labourers, as Charkham termed it, and needed to consider
how the results and recommendations of others could

be successfully integrated with its own.[1] It was hardly surprising, given the high level of interest in and expectations of the Committee, that suggestions had already been sent in to the secretariat (as Peace noted in early June), principally from senior figures in the accountancy profession, about what the Committee should consider.[2]

June 1991: Deciding How To Do It

Traditionally committees in the UK (as elsewhere) gathered evidence and opinions in two ways, through written submissions made to them and by taking formal oral evidence at meetings, where witnesses could be questioned. The Radcliffe Committee, for example, charged with inquiring into the working of the UK's monetary system in 1957 (it reported in 1959), took formal oral evidence at 59 of its 88 meetings, questioning in all 200 witnesses (Capie 2010: 100). This procedure followed the pattern developed in the more leisurely times of the nineteenth-century inquiries, but by the second half of the twentieth century it seems that most official or semi-official committees were looking for less time-consuming ways of exploring the issues on

---

[1] The phrase was used by Jonathan Charkham in a letter to Adrian Cadbury, 8 July 1991: 'As you have noted, we shall be working at a time when numerous others, often experts, are labouring in a vineyard' (CAD 01061). Charkham was concerned about how the outputs of the various groups might be effectively integrated, and this later became a significant problem: see Chapter 5.

[2] CAD 01255. The profession did not always speak with a single voice: see CAD 01161, letter from Chapman at Arthur Andersen.

which they had been asked to report. The Committee on Turnover Taxation (the Richardson Committee), for example, appointed in April 1963 and reporting in March 1964, gave a questionnaire to its chosen representative seventeen business organizations, using the responses as the basis for the oral evidence it then took from them (Rollings 2007: 228–40). But a questionnaire could not hope to capture the varied and nuanced views that existed in the constituencies concerned with corporate governance. Nor would there be time for the meetings to take oral evidence, given that it was proving difficult enough to find dates on which all members could attend the monthly meetings, because of their existing commitments. With no predecessor inquiry offering a perfect template for the Committee, the chairman and secretary had to develop their own modus operandi.

It was originally envisaged that the Committee would produce and publish a draft and code by the end of the year.[3] This short timetable did not allow for a great deal of public consultation before the publication of the draft Report, since it was anticipated that most of that would follow publication and the responses would be taken into account in shaping the final Report. However, as Cadbury and Peace were preparing the Committee's schedule, Peace noted that he had already received calls from groups and individuals who were eager to influence the Committee's thinking; he wrote to Cadbury: 'I think we should make our terms of reference known

[3] CAD 01181. See also Peace's letter of 12 June: 'subject to discussion at the first meeting…the intention will be to produce an interim report for public consultation by the end of December.'

when they are finalised and give those who are keen to give us their views the opportunity to do so.'[4] At that time the terms of reference, drafted at the end of April, were broadly outlined, and the changes that were made evolved gradually through the meetings to achieve the more focused version that appeared in the draft Report and—unchanged—in the final Report (see Appendix 2).

With this in mind, in June Cadbury wrote to a number of chairmen and chief executives of major companies soliciting their views. Among these, many of whom he knew personally through his and their interests in governance, was Neville Bain, chief executive of the Coats Viyella Group. His response, while noting the problems with audit, highlighted what he called the broader issue of the evaluation of a company's progress in terms that were to be echoed in many of the submissions and evidence given to the Committee through the autumn of 1991. Lack of common accounting standards, evidenced in the failures of Polly Peck and Coloroll (both went into receivership in 1990), he suggested, should be dealt with by the accounting bodies. More generally, 'appropriate corporate governance', he wrote, needed 'a strong independent presence of non-executive directors led by a Chairman whose role is not amalgamated or confused with that of the Chief Executive'. The audit committee, he concluded, needed more time and teeth.[5] These and other views presented over the autumn in the informal

---

[4] CAD 01149.
[5] CAD 01045.

discussions Cadbury undertook (they were recorded by Peace) formed part of a much more extensive consultation than anticipated, but played a role in enriching both the Committee's understanding and its deliberations.

In preparation for the first meeting of the Committee, Peace, in close consultation with Cadbury, drafted a set of documents that provided the basis for steering the work of the Committee.[6] There was a briefing paper that included a comprehensive summary of recent publications on roles and responsibilities of directors, shareholders, and auditors. It noted current studies underway within the accountancy profession by ICAS, APB, ICAEW (both its Financial Reporting and Auditing Group and its Research Board), as well as other related work being undertaken by the CBI's steering group on long termism and corporate governance, the ISC, the FRC, the Institutional Fund Managers Association, and the Hundred Group of finance directors.[7]

As part of this package, Peace designed an outline structure for the proposed code of best practice,[8] noting its resemblance to the Australian code, described as

[6] CAD 01149.

[7] Although it was not mentioned in this briefing paper, the Committee's secretariat received around this time a memorandum from the Royal Society for the Encouragement of Arts, Manufactures and Commerce (RSA) on a proposal it was developing to explore the 'Purpose of the Company' through a series of seminars and discussions. Its objectives went much further and wider than the Committee's remit and it resulted in the report 'Tomorrow's Company: The Role of Business in a Changing World', published in 1995. CAD 01035 and CAD 01027.

[8] He also referred to it as the 'recommended code'.

principles for 'corporate practices and conduct'[9] published earlier in the year. He pointed out, however, that the Australian code had a greater emphasis on ethics and conduct than his outline, which focused on information flows and shareholder responsibilities. The notion of a code, flagged at the launch, had been around for some time,[10] but Cadbury needed to secure the Committee members' agreement to its inclusion in the Report. Peace suggested a suitable form of words for the first meeting:

As for our report, the Committee may agree that a major element should be a code which pulls together the work being done in our field and clarifies the relationships between the various interests. If it would be helpful we could ask the Secretary to prepare a draft framework for the code for the next meeting of the Committee and as it were to fill in the framework as we go along, presenting to each of our meetings a fuller draft which reflects discussion at our last meeting.[11]

In the event this proposal was accepted at the first meeting, the draft framework was approved at the second meeting, and was added to thereafter as the areas were discussed and the wording approved. It was a useful way of recording decisions, and the Committee clearly found it a helpful way of proceeding, since the same process was used in revising the draft Report.

---

[9] CAD 01029.
[10] The CBI's Watkinson Report had suggested a Code of Corporate Conduct in 1973.
[11] CAD 01149.

Charkham, while expressing his admiration for the work carried out in June, was less than enthusiastic about a code, fearing it would tend to the lowest common denominator. But, in a letter to Cadbury, he suggested the production of a framework setting out the relationships and responsibilities within the corporate informational network: this he saw as the Committee's main task. It would enable the slotting-in of references to work being done by other groups, since he recognized the difficulty of achieving consensus among all the groups.[12] By the end of June Peace had set out a detailed work programme identifying the areas to be addressed at each of the planned meetings, noting: 'The thought which struck me rather forcefully as I drew up the outline was that we shall need to share the work about a bit!'[13] Members of the Committee were to be asked to lead discussions and perhaps also prepare papers and notes on the matters in which their knowledge and expertise lay.

Initial Meetings with the Committee Members (and Others)

Before the first formal meeting of the Committee in July, Cadbury met most of the members of the Committee individually;[14] this was both as a matter of courtesy, as

[12] CAD 01061.
[13] CAD 01149.
[14] There is no record of interviews at this time with two members, Andrew Likierman and Mark Sheldon.

well as to probe where each of them might stand on some of the potentially contentious issues discussed later in this chapter. As Cadbury noted, in a letter to Neville Bain: 'I do not, as yet, know where the sympathies of my fellow members... lie.'[15] The first of these meetings—which shed some interesting light on the expectations and opinions of the Committee members—was with Ron Dearing, 'to canvas [his] view on the ground which the committee might cover'.[16] Four areas were highlighted in Dearing's response to this: the role of the non-executive directors, auditors, annual reports, and the institutional investors. He did not mince his words in describing the present situation; companies, he suggested 'did not get value out of their non-executive directors', who were often poorly selected. Auditors 'were in a fundamentally weak position', and they 'needed to be both frightened and strengthened', while the standard of annual reports was 'very poor', all ample reasons for the role the FRC had played in the establishment of the Committee. The FRC itself, he noted, was working on a report (to be produced in November) on the quality of financial reporting and how it could be improved.

Cadbury's initial interview with Andrew Hugh Smith covered much the same ground but elicited slightly different responses. Hugh Smith said he saw the Committee 'as set up to address the middle ground in the corporate governance debate', that being where he

---

[15] CAD 01045.
[16] CAD 01225.

placed the responsibilities of the auditor as well as those of the director and communications with the shareholder. He highlighted the conflict between disclosure and sensible commercial confidentiality as a significant one and went on to say that, while he did not envisage that the report should be built on a programme of proposals for legislative change, he would not object if it identified some desirable amendments for the next routine update of the Companies Act.[17] Dearing and Hugh Smith represented two of the sponsoring bodies of the Committee, and these early discussions played a part in defining and establishing not only the remit of the Committee but also its boundaries. The scope of the initial remit was so wide that the problem of defining more closely what the Committee should—and indeed could—cover was exercising the minds of Cadbury and Peace as they worked on the draft structures of the Report and the Code.

The members on the Committee from the accounting bodies, who had played such a significant role in its setting up, also met Cadbury in June. Nigel Macdonald, who was chairing the ICAS working party, was anxious to ensure coordination between the two groups. The ICAS terms of reference defined three specific aspects to be explored: management responsibility for financial statements, internal control systems, and audit

---

[17] CAD 01259, 26 June 1991.
[18] CAD 01223, 14 June, meeting with Nigel Macdonald, with ICAS terms of reference attached.

committees.[18] While all of these had some overlap with Cadbury's remit—as did research then underway at the ICAEW—Macdonald wanted ICAS to be given credit for its work, while its results should also be 'embraced' by the Committee.[19] A much shorter discussion was held on 19 June between Cadbury and Jim Butler, then senior partner of KPMG Peat Marwick McLintock. Reiterating the unanimous support of the eight leading accountancy firms for the Committee's establishment, he suggested that the chairmen of the various working groups noted in the early briefing paper should be invited, in due course, to present their findings to the Committee. Audit committees and directors' pay were the two topic areas he mentioned as particularly lacking in clarity.[20]

Two other senior heads of accountancy firms had similar early discussions with Cadbury at this time, Brandon Gough, senior partner of Coopers & Lybrand Deloitte, and Chris Swinson, partner in BDO Binder Hamlyn. Gough's concerns were centred on auditors and the criticisms they were attracting, some of which he thought to be fair and some not. Accounting standards allowed too much leeway, he thought, citing the recent case of Polly Peck: in its treatment of currency transactions, the company had stayed within the standard, but the standard had not made sense in the context of a high inflation country. Clarity and toughness were needed about who was responsible for what, as well as about what was a

---

[19] CAD 01223.
[20] CAD 01245.

reasonable level of expectation of the audit.[21] Some two weeks later Gough followed up the discussion with a letter noting the results of his own discussions on what should be the key issues for the Committee with a group of senior partners at Coopers & Lybrand Deloitte. These he identified as the roles of non-executive directors and shareholders, unforeseen company failures, inadequate internal controls and auditor appointment, and remuneration,[22] all matters already included on the agendas for the Committee's meetings. Swinson's discussion with Cadbury and Peace ranged more widely over the problems of financial reporting and auditing, the subject of a current study by the ICAEW's Financial Reporting and Auditing Group. The profession, he said, was strongly opposed to the views of those who wanted auditors to report more widely on forecasts: 'auditors did not want to be required to take a view in areas where one man's prudent judgement was another man's recklessness'.[23]

The meetings that Cadbury had with the remaining members of the Committee at this time revealed the different perspectives and expectations they brought to the Committee's table. Jonathan Charkham's views reflected his long and close involvement through the 1980s with the developing corporate governance lobby. His discussion with Cadbury indicated a keen awareness of the wider issues in both the UK and the USA.

---

[21] CAD 01219.
[22] CAD 01055.
[23] CAD 01254.

In fact it was at this time that a US Working Group on Corporate Governance published its first statement of principles on how to reconcile the tensions between owners and managers.[24] Despite the general tendency to refer to 'Anglo-American' capitalism as one type, there were considerable differences in governance between the two countries, and the statement does not seem to have been accorded a great deal of attention in the UK. In his discussion with Cadbury, Charkham suggested that the Committee's 'fundamental concern' was the 'passage of information...that held all the parties in the system together'. That led to questions as to who should supply the information—it was, he thought, the directors' responsibility—as well as the form in which such information should be conveyed. Responding to a question from Cadbury as to how changes could be made, Charkham argued that 'ultimately it would be for the DTI to establish the regulatory framework by statutory means. He believed that it was a proper role for government to establish what was in effect the price for limited liability.'[25] This was not a view shared by all the members of the Committee, nor by many outside parties.

---

[24] 'A New Compact for Owners and Directors', *Harvard Business Review* (July–August 1991) 141–3. In the November–December issue of the *Harvard Business Review* three commentators discussed the principles and their use; one of the commentators was Lord Hanson, chairman of Hanson plc, an Anglo-US corporation, later a keen critic of the Committee's Report, as demonstrated in a speech he made to the Worshipful Company of Actuaries, reported in the *Sunday Telegraph*, 12 July 1992.

[25] CAD 01253.

Hugh Collum drew attention to the international diversity of accounting standards, noting that he saw the Committee as being offered a 'a window of opportunity' to reduce some of that diversity.[26] He went on to say that 'if the UK could get its accounting act right then it would be able to take the lead in Europe'. His discussion with Cadbury then moved on, firstly, to defining the boundaries between auditors and directors, and, secondly, to the question of how much detail of a company's future plans should be revealed. Collum's reference to Europe reflected the increasing integration of British business with that of Europe after two decades of British membership of the EU, as well as the growth across the world of what is generally called 'globalization'. That the international dimensions of any change in corporate governance in the UK were significant was recognized by Cadbury and other members of the Committee, as well as in some of the submissions to the Committee, and became part of the basis of its deliberations. As Cadbury wrote to Charkham, after their interview, 'one point we do need to keep in mind when considering what should appear in reports is that the larger companies are addressing an international audience...Ought we not to recognise that companies nowadays are owned and operated internationally?'[27]

While Charkham and Collum both showed an enthusiasm for the Committee and its purpose, some reservations

---

[26] CAD 01243.
[27] CAD 01013.

on these matters emerged in Cadbury's discussions with three other members of the Committee, Sir Dermot de Trafford, Ian Butler, and Mike Sandland. De Trafford represented the Institute of Directors on the Committee. Traditionally conservative in its approach, the organization has been described in the early 1990s as one where 'the desire for minimalist government, stripped down to "law and order, low taxes, sound money" remains undimmed' (Boswell and Peters 1997: 164). Sir Dermot was reluctant, it seems, to enter into wider discussion. He would, he told Cadbury, 'expect to obtain his Council's approval to any position which the IOD took on the work of the committee'.[28] Ian Butler from the CBI told Cadbury that his principal area of concern was the expectation that had developed that information would be 'smoothed' between company management and analysts. He found the pressure in the media for companies to be more forthcoming to be 'unattractive and dangerous'. Moreover, he pointed out that increased disclosure requirements would lead to more problems and costs for companies.[29]

A week after this meeting, as already arranged, Cadbury and Peace, escorted by Butler, attended a meeting of the CBI Steering Group on Corporate Governance. Cadbury spoke briefly to introduce the Committee and its purpose, before the meeting moved on to discuss its main business of the day, the CBI response to the recent

---

[28] CAD 01255.
[29] CAD 01249.

discussion paper produced by the ABI on the role of the institutional shareholders. From the discussion and from the CBI's official response document (approved by its National Council on 26 June) there arose several points that were to resurface regularly in the Committee's dealings with the CBI throughout its deliberations. The first of these was that the CBI, stressing the importance of flexibility, favoured 'broad principles for guidance' rather than 'tightly drawn rules and codes'. The second was that, while fully supporting the view that 'non-executive directors bring valued expertise of a particular nature to the board...we are against hard and fast rules on the composition of the board'. Finally, on the appointment of audit and remuneration committees, the response noted:

Our approach is to say that the appointment of such committees would be a matter for boards to decide in the light of the individual company's circumstances. We restate our concern that to prescribe one group of directors should exclusively supervise or monitor the activity of others will lead to a two-tier structure which is alien to the UK's conception of a unitary board.[30]

The last of Cadbury's meetings with Committee members was with Mike Sandland of the Institutional Shareholders' Committee, which took place early in the day on which the first meeting of the Committee was to be held. Sandland began the meeting by admitting that his initial doubts about the Committee's establishment

---

[30] CAD 01077.

had been 'somewhat' modified.[31] He did, however, stress that he did not want the Committee to attempt too much, suggesting that the terms of reference should be 'adjusted' to emphasize that the Committee would be concentrating on the financial aspects of the subject. The ISC, which had published a statement in April on best practice on the roles and duties of directors, was now working on a new paper on the responsibilities of the institutional shareholders, which would be completed in the autumn. He could report on progress to the Committee's September meeting.

The First Meeting and its Aftermath

The first meeting of the Committee was held at 4 p.m. on 15 July at Chartered Accountants' Hall in Moorgate Place. The agenda, designed by Cadbury and Peace earlier in the month, began with a consideration of the Committee's purpose and terms of reference. Notes on these had been circulated beforehand, together with two other papers drafted by Peace, one on recent relevant publications and studies in progress and one on the roles and responsibilities of shareholders, directors, and auditors. Inevitably, the discussion ranged widely and generally across the agenda items,[32] not least the Committee's terms of reference, given that, as we have noted above, some members wanted a narrow interpretation of its

---

[31] CAD 11221.
[32] Interviewee S.

purpose while others anticipated a broader and more inclusive approach. That this latter view prevailed is clear from correspondence with the DTI, whose observer on the Committee, Sarah Brown, noted 'the Committee's wish to consider some issues about the constitution of company boards and the role of major shareholders which go rather wider than strictly "financial aspects"'.[33] The Committee's sense of purpose may well have been sharpened by recent events: on 5 July the City's regulators, headed by the Bank of England, closed down the worldwide operations of the Bank of Credit and Commerce International (BCCI), in the wake of a Price Waterhouse report completed in June, which gave detailed evidence of large frauds by BCCI officials over a number of years.[34]

The Committee agreed the schedule of work for the autumn, the meetings, and their agendas. They also agreed that the draft framework for a code of practice, prepared by Peace, should be tabled at each meeting and 'filled out as the committee's work progresses'.[35] This, as Peace himself had noted, would be 'a useful means of focusing the discussion in that it would concentrate the committee's mind on reaching conclusions that could be reflected in the code'.[36] Although it was initially described

---

[33] CAD 01097.

[34] Price Waterhouse Sandstorm Report for the Bank of England, June 1991. Not available in the UK, but parts available in the USA can be found on the website of the Association for Accountancy and Business Affairs <http://visar.csustan.edu/aaba/BCCISandstormRelease.html> (accessed 12 December 2012).

[35] CAD 01149.

[36] CAD 01149.

as a code of recommended practice, 'which would command widespread support' (see Appendix 2), Cadbury's own reflection a month later was that, although such a code was the objective the Committee had been charged with producing, 'for the time being [we] have adopted the more general objective of recommendations on best practice'.[37] The difference between these is not entirely clear, since the criteria for deciding what was 'good' practice (the word used in the final version of the terms of reference) and 'best' practice do not seem to have been explicitly stated.

There was no meeting in August, but Cadbury and Peace continued to work for the rest of July and much of August, dealing with submissions that came in, continuing to take oral evidence, and preparing for the September meeting. At the end of the month the papers for the September meeting were circulated. A number of members could not attend this meeting but gave their views on paper. Among the many issues emerging there was one that merits a brief discussion at this stage. This was the question of whether or not there was a case for making statutory provision for some of the Committee's recommendations. Hugh Smith had, as we have seen, excluded special legislation while allowing for some amendments to the existing Companies Act, when it was next revised. Others, who had for so long been advocating a larger role in governance for non-executive directors,

---

[37] CAD 01299.

had begun to favour legislation. For example, Charkham wrote to Cadbury early in September with comments on the agenda for that month's meeting, which he could not attend, concluding with the statement: 'I must record that I have now reluctantly come to the view that legislation to make independent directors necessary for public companies would be helpful.'[38] In his written submission, Lord Ezra[39] had also supported the notion of statutory provision for non-executive directors, suggesting that, without 'legislative back-up',[40] the change would be very slow. However, at much the same time a letter from Sarah Brown at the DTI (who also could not attend the September meeting) made clear the view from the government (and presumably the then incumbent minister at the DTI, Peter Lilley) that, as she put it, 'non-executives are only useful if they are well-informed and independent-minded and these are not qualities for which you can legislate'.[41] The DTI must also have been well aware that neither the CBI nor the IoD were likely to support such legislation, despite what Ezra described as 'a growing consensus' in favour of the proposal.

Brown also issued two further warnings on the tasks that the Committee would be unwise to tackle: the first was any attempt to define the responsibility of

---

[38] CAD 01099.

[39] Derek Ezra had a long career with the National Coal Board (1947–82) and was its chairman from 1971 to 1982. In the 1980s he was a Liberal Party front-bench spokesman in the House of Lords (Boswell and Peters 1997: 229).

[40] CAD 01075.

[41] CAD 01097.

directors—it was a task at which many had failed, and she concluded: 'I am sure it is not something the Committee should take on.' The second was the problem of directors' remuneration, a matter that had attracted a good deal of media criticism in the period before the Committee was appointed and raised expectations that it would be part of its remit. Brown wrote:

On directors' remuneration, I am sure the Committee should be cautious about how far it goes but it *might* want to comment on what kind of measures are appropriate for determining performance pay (or more probably what kind are not)...Especially given the potential link with financial reporting, the Committee might at least want to debate this point.[42]

The September 1991 Meeting

For its second meeting on 11 September, the Committee met for the first time at the Bank of England, where a portrait of the influential former Governor, Montagu Norman, gazed down on them.[43] It was a smaller meeting, as three members were unable to attend, Charkham, Collum, and Macdonald, as well as Brown. Those present discussed first the framework code (it was approved and added to), secondly the roles and responsibilities of shareholders (with an introduction by Sandland of the ISC), thirdly audit committees, and fourthly the role of

---

[42] CAD 01097.
[43] Interviewee L.

non-executive directors. It was, according to Cadbury's note to Committee members after the meeting, 'a difficult agenda',[44] and the deliberations on these topics were neither definitive nor conclusive—they were all revisited in meetings over the following months. The note makes clear some of the problems emerging in the discussions: 'I accept that our discussions will have a clearer focus, as soon as we can decide on the form which our draft report is likely to take,' he wrote, adding that, 'whatever form our recommendations take, we will need to include proposals for putting them into effect, monitoring them and keeping them up to date. It will be for those who set us up, or the wider constituency involved through the members of the Committee, to decide what action to take on our findings.' Before going on to summarize the conclusions, as he saw them, on non-executive directors, Cadbury made two other significant points relating to the approach the Committee would adopt in preparing the draft Report and Code: the first concerned principles, the second the Committee's remit:

there would seem to be advantages in basing our recommendations...on broad principles. The reasons include the constraints of time, not overlapping with others in the field and avoiding being drawn into more and more detail (trying to define 'non-executive directors' or 'independent directors', for example). At the same time, we could usefully draw attention

---

[44] In a memo to members after the meeting. CAD 01299, 21 September 1991.

to the main sources of guidance to which those concerned could turn in interpreting our recommendations.

A statement of principles can be reasonably brief and it can be required to be followed in spirit, rather than evaded through the small print. It can also insist that substance rules over form. I recognise the concern that the outcome may sound platitudinous, but we should not, in my view worry too much about this. First, if our principles were to be revolutionary they would be unlikely either to be sound or enforceable. Second, it is making the principles stick which is important...

We do have to keep continually in mind that our remit is limited to the financial aspects of corporate governance... I think it is essential to start by establishing the Board framework within which such later items as audit committees and internal financial controls will have to fit.[45]

October–December 1991: Shaping the Report and the Code

Over this period the chairman and secretary had much to do in preparing for the monthly meetings,[46] and in drafting the papers that embodied not only the ongoing research outside the Committee but also the relevant ideas and suggestions in the submissions that continued to arrive at the secretariat. As Peace had noted in June, there was a great deal of ground to cover, and the burden

---

[45] In a memo to members after the meeting. CAD 01299, 21 September 1991.

[46] Held on 17 October, 13 November, and 18 December.

of doing so fell inevitably on the chairman and secretary. They also had a busy programme, continuing the informal interviews that had begun in June. Among these, Cadbury had discussions with a number of financial directors, including those of the Pearson Group and Trust Houses Forte, and with chairmen of large corporations, including Sir Simon Hornby of W. H. Smith. Among the issues Cadbury discussed with Hornby, who had himself been a non-executive on the Pearson board of directors, were two that were proving to be of particular and significant difficulty to the Committee. The first of these was the problem of getting institutional shareholders 'to think of themselves as owners'. Hornby was frank in noting that some of his company's long-term investors—he instanced the Prudential and Standard Life—were less equivocal about ownership than others who did not see themselves as owners and who, if dissatisfied, would simply sell up and buy into another company. On auditors too, Hornby was similarly outspoken: 'finance directors had auditors in their pockets, because auditors were too afraid of losing the account'. Auditors, he said, should report to the audit committee, not the finance director, and the chairman of the audit committee should be paid more than the standard non-executive rate in recognition of the extra work.[47]

The only politician who was interviewed was the Opposition spokeswoman on Corporate and City affairs, Marjorie Mowlam, who presented Cadbury with the

---

[47] CAD 01171.

Labour Party's policy on regulation of financial matters, saying bluntly: 'if the Committee's report ducked the basic issues, it would be hammered.' She did not want a 'waffly report with no teeth.' She did, however, write to Cadbury a few days later to thank him for his time and a 'useful' meeting, adding: 'One point I did mean to raise in our discussion relating to non-executive directors was the number of women. I would dearly like to see this increase.'[48] Further light was shed on the life of non-executive directors by the meeting Cadbury had in September with Dennis Stevenson, who held three non-executive posts, one with Manpower, formerly Blue Arrow.[49] He argued that the financial recompense 'bore no relation to the onerous duties involved'.[50] There was also a meeting with James Leek, a director of Caparo Industries plc, who put his case to Cadbury for legal reform of auditors' liability, in the wake of the Caparo decision in the courts.[51] On this highly controversial matter the Committee, much to the disappointment of many, did not urge reform in either the draft or the final Report. Its rationale for defending the status quo was set out in an appendix to the final Report, drafted by the lawyer on the Committee, Mark Sheldon.[52]

---

[48] CAD 01239.

[49] Senior executives of the merchant bank County Natwest were accused of inflating the success of a rights issue of Blue Arrow shares by selling shares in non-arm's-length transactions (see Chapter 1).

[50] CAD 01029.

[51] CAD 010201.

[52] See Appendix to the Report (Cadbury 1992).

Through the autumn, Cadbury's schedule also included regular speaking engagements at functions such as, for example, a dinner at Claridge's early in October, where he talked to a group of senior executives over dinner about the role of the chairman.[53] In early November he attended a dinner given by the accountancy firm Pannell Kerr Forster, where he spoke about corporate governance; at around the same time he attended and spoke at some length at the PIRC conference, as well as addressing the CBI's national conference.[54]

There were few submissions from individual shareholders, but that is, perhaps, hardly surprising; the CBI estimate of individual shareholders in 1989 stood at just 20 per cent of all shareholders.[55] One who did write into the Committee noted his dissatisfaction with directors' contracts and the arrangements for remuneration,[56] a matter already on the agenda. That individual shareholders in many companies felt disadvantaged, not least by the quantity and quality of the information supplied to them—in contrast to that available to institutional shareholders—was a point made in the submission of Dr Maurice Gillibrand. A scientist who had long worked for ICI and a former secretary of the Association of Professional Scientists and Technologists, Gillibrand had also been involved with the UK Shareholders' Association, and his submission argued the urgent need

[53] CAD 01109, letter from Sir Denys Henderson, chairman of ICI.
[54] CAD 03231.
[55] CAD 03261.
[56] CAD 01119, letter from Simon Blunt.

for reform of communication between boards, shareholders, and other stakeholders.[57]

It was in October, possibly at the October meeting, that the schedule for the publication of the draft Report and Code was changed. At that meeting the recommendations on non-executive directors were agreed, but the Committee still had much to discuss and decide on what recommendations it would make on audit. Although a useful memo had been submitted by the Financial Reporting and Auditing Group of the ICAEW,[58] it had been agreed that the results of the ICAS working group would be absorbed into the draft Report and Code. However, ICAS now acknowledged that its work, expected in late October, would not be completed until February. In Cadbury's speech to the PIRC conference on 13 November, he suggested that the draft Report and Code would be published in March 1992.[59] This decision had not been made public when, early in November, the news reached London of the death of Robert Maxwell on 5 November at sea, off the coast of Tenerife. The Committee met on 13 November, eight days after this. While speculation was rife about the nature of Maxwell's demise—accident or suicide dominated the headlines—of more immediate concern to the Committee was the unravelling of his business empire, built up by acquisitions in the 1980s. Earlier in 1991 the Mirror Group Newspapers (MGN), which Maxwell had bought in 1984, had been floated as a public company,

[57] CAD 02237.
[58] CAD 03112.
[59] CAD 01166.

but after his death it soon emerged that that its debts far outweighed its assets and that some £440m were missing from its pension fund.[60] These revelations of disastrous finances and mismanagement, combined with fraud, focused attention once again on the Committee, leading in turn to greater expectations of the Committee's Report and recommendations. The Committee's response, according to Cadbury, was to look again more closely at the areas of board responsibility and composition. To go further was beyond its remit. Memories are notoriously short, and Maxwell had been surprisingly successful in burying the findings of the 1970 DTI report when, in the wake of the Pergamon–Leasco affair, he was described as a person who could not be relied upon 'to exercise proper stewardship of a publicly quoted company'.[61] When Cadbury was asked about Maxwell in an interview with Lisa Buckingham for the *Guardian* in March 1992, his reply reflected this history: 'You have to remember with Maxwell there was a DTI report in the public domain and everyone knew it.'[62]

It may not have been coincidental that late in November an eighteen-page submission arrived at the Committee's office. Written by two Labour MPs, Jim Cousins and Austin Mitchell, with an academic, Prem Sikka, it was highly critical of the composition and

---

[60] Maxwell Communication Corporation plc. International Directory of Company Histories 1993, St James Press, vol. 7.

[61] Quoted in the DTI investigation into Mirror Group Newspapers plc <http://www.pixunlimited.co.uk/Media/pdf/mirrorgroup.pdf> (accessed 12 December 2012).

[62] *Guardian*, 15 March 1992.

purpose of the Committee and of what it described as the UK's 'casino capitalism'. Based on the polemical paper the authors had written and the Fabian Society had published earlier in the year,[63] it appears to be the only submission to argue in favour of the EU's Fifth Directive (vigorously opposed by the CBI and the IoD), which would extend the two-tier board common in Europe to the UK. The submission contained twenty-one specific recommendations on audit, and was clearly read and annotated by Cadbury himself.[64] It was also summarized by Peace as part of a paper he prepared with the proposals that had been made on auditors for the deliberations at the Committee's December meeting.[65]

As the results produced by the 'labourers in the vine-yard' started to trickle in—the Hundred Group submitted its study in December—the work of integration became more complex and required more synthesis. In December and early January this formed part of the preparation for a two-day retreat planned for January. For that purpose Cadbury himself prepared a ten-page document on standards of financial reporting and of auditing. In this he set out clearly the grounds for concern, the causes, and the position of auditors, summarizing the evidence from the submissions, both formal and informal. He went on to outline the remedies, in terms of action by the profession and by companies and the role for the Committee.[66]

[63] *Accounting for Change* (Fabian Society, August 1991).
[64] CAD 01148.
[65] CAD 03115.
[66] CAD 01301.

By early December the rounds of meetings, both of the Committee and outside it, as well as his speaking engagements and extensive informal discussions, had led Cadbury to question the Committee's purpose and the nature of its engagement with the problems. In a meeting with Andrew Likierman on 3 December he articulated his concern in these terms: that 'he was concerned that the Committee should agree on *what* it was addressing, and *why*. He was convinced there was a problem, but defining it was not easy.' In the course of the discussion that followed, Likierman argued that there were problems, but the Committee needed to avoid the areas that were the province of the FRC and the APB and go for focused recommendations in particular areas.[67] At the same time Cadbury wrote to the Committee's sponsors—the Stock Exchange, the FRC, and the accounting bodies—posing similar questions as to whether the Committee was addressing what it had been intended to do. The answer seems to have been reassuring—that the Committee was basically on the right lines.[68]

January–April 1992: Towards Publication

The Committee met for a two-day 'retreat' towards the end of January 1992. A number of papers had been circulated in advance, covering a variety of topics to be

---

[67] CAD 01163.
[68] CAD 01139.

included in the Report and Code, including the roles and responsibilities of shareholders, internal control, opinion shopping, directors' remuneration, internal audit, and audit committees, as well as what was described as 'a skeleton draft report'.[69] All members except Hugh Collum attended, and he spent some time with Cadbury earlier in January, giving his views on the papers and proposals circulated. He agreed with many of the suggestions but strongly opposed the idea of quarterly reports. He added that, given the heavy duties being placed on non-executive directors, the Committee might recommend 'a specific minimum'. His final comment was: 'It was hard to argue against the emerging recommendations, but if it all happened it was going to involve a great deal of extra work and bureaucracy!'[70] This was a view that became all too familiar to Committee members after the publication of the draft Report.

Even at this relatively late stage in the Committee's deliberations, submissions continued to be accepted, read, and considered. In January and February the Gillibrand submission, discussed above, arrived, as did one from Dick Taverne,[71] who argued that the problem lay with the institutional shareholders, and suggested that a new form

[69] CAD 01159.
[70] CAD 01159.
[71] Dick Taverne (born 1928). A Labour MP 1962–72, he left the party in 1972, standing as an Independent at Lincoln, where he won the seat. He later joined the Social Democrat Party and then the Liberal Democrats. He founded the Institute for Fiscal Studies in 1979, and became a life peer in 1996.

of Investors Relations Committee should be established.[72] And on 12 March the CBI sent in a memorandum, reiterating the views it had already presented to Cadbury and the Committee.[73] Following its January retreat, the Committee met in February, with progress being made with both the Report and the Code, as well as the integration of the findings of the ICAS working party. By then, however, a general election was looming. The difficulty of publishing at such a time was well described by Lord Watkinson, an old friend and colleague of Cadbury, in a letter at the beginning of February. He wrote:

May I say that March will be a politically fraught month. Your report might well get a good deal of notice if published then, but I wonder if it will not be savaged by both parties, for perhaps different reasons. They will be at one another's throats by then. It is of course nothing to do with me but I do wonder if it could be better used as a lever if published soon after the Election (probably April)...when the new government will be looking for 'good things to do'...Please do not think that I am trying to tell you what to do, but I would like to see the report make a real impact, it is so badly needed.[74]

We do not know whether it was his advice or the Committee's own judgement, but publication was delayed until May.

---

[72] CAD 02235.
[73] CAD 03261.
[74] CAD 01260. Watkinson's cynicism about politicians may well have derived from his own time in politics and from suffering in Macmillan's 'night of the long knives'.

The Committee's last meeting before publication was held on 23 March. It was a long and arduous meeting, at least in Charkham's view; he wrote to Cadbury the day after noting: 'You must feel quite drained after yesterday but I thought we made excellent progress.'[75] Ron Dearing, too, wrote to Cadbury the same day, principally to pick up on a brief discussion at the end of the meeting when it had been mooted that the Committee should think about areas of vulnerability, in the shape of criticisms that might be made of the Report and Code. Dearing began by counting his 'blessings':

My own motivation as a co-sponsor of the Cadbury Committee was to strengthen the position of the auditor and to get the responsibilities of directors into clear focus. In those terms the draft report is excellent and will do much good. Even if it did no more the Committee would have made an important contribution that was much needed. And of course it has done more.

He went on to note that a critic might argue that, in terms of improving corporate accountability, the Committee had focused on the needs of large institutional shareholders and had paid little attention to employees or ordinary shareholders. He suggested that the importance of employees might be acknowledged by a provision in the Code that companies should publish 'a special publication for the workforce'. Meeting the needs of ordinary shareholders had apparently been discussed by the Committee with little enthusiasm: he observed that

[75] CAD 03249.

'there was no one at the meeting, apart from yourself with some support from myself, who felt the game was worth a candle'. Dearing suggested that AGMs could be made more 'shareholder friendly' by encouraging shareholders to submit questions in advance, a practice that had been introduced by ICI, according to Gillibrand's submission,[76] and that has since become commonplace in large companies. Developing this idea, Dearing proposed that questions could be selected by a specially constituted shareholder committee. He concluded: 'You may have better ideas and I can imagine the committee groaning about the idea, but if we face up to the fact that, to the great mass of ordinary people, accounts are incomprehensible; that the AGM is an intimidating occasion for the ordinary man or woman, and that they do have a legitimate interest, to do nothing would I think be a legitimate basis for criticising our proposal in terms of our own proclaimed objective of improving accountability.'[77]

Over the next month, the Report and the Code were finalized for publication. They were presented as an integrated document; the Report had seven sections, starting with an explanation of its setting, followed by an introduction detailing the Committee's sponsors, its rationale, and the nature of corporate governance. The third section discussed the Code and compliance with it, leading into a long fourth section on the board. Auditing was

---

[76] CAD 02237.
[77] CAD 01293.

dealt with in section five and shareholders in section six, with a brief conclusion. A summary of the report's recommendations preceded the presentation of the Code of Best Practice, set out on two pages with cross references to the relevant paragraphs of the main Report for each of the code's constituents.

At the same time, in the preparation for the launch of the draft Report, Peace brought together suggestions on the areas of vulnerability made at the meeting—Dearing noted that Likierman had produced ten.[78] These, together with others suggested in the days following the meeting—including a list from the ICAEW—were circulated and revised, with draft responses. By 22 May the members of the Committee were armed for the press launch with a briefing of twenty-one potential questions, which, it was envisaged, might be asked, and the answers to them. These covered many areas, including representation on the Committee, whether the Report gave too favourable treatment to some interests over others—large shareholders, small companies, and auditors were mentioned—and the enforcement of the Code.[79] The draft Report and Code were published at the end of May, with the press briefing held on 26 May. How they were received we shall explore in the next chapter.

---

[78] CAD 01293.
[79] CAD 01287.

4

From the Draft to the Final Report

The draft Report received extensive newspaper coverage in the days immediately following its publication and presentation to the press on 26 May. It soon became clear that this was no nine-day wonder, as the newspapers continued to follow the story with discussion of the draft's proposals throughout the period designated for consultation (until the end of July) and beyond. While some comment in the broadsheets and business press had been foreseen, this was much more attention than the Committee had anticipated and, according to Cadbury himself, it also played a part in generating 'a level of response to the invitation to comment [directly to the Committee] beyond our expectations'.[1] Since the Committee's establishment the year before and while its deliberations had been taking place, corporate governance had become, according to the Governor of the Bank

[1] Cadbury's review of responses to the draft Report, presented to Committee meeting, September 1992. Additional papers.

of England, 'fashionable'.[2] Partly because of continuing corporate problems at a time of recession and partly because of the publicity the Committee's members, especially its chairman, had achieved by writing and speaking publicly on the subject, corporate governance had a higher public profile. Interest, therefore, in what the Committee might prescribe for the UK's corporate ailments was running high, ramped up by the well-publicized concerns about the Maxwell affair as well as the issues of the high salaries and rewards enjoyed by senior managers and directors. The latter was one of the two issues that, according to Dearing, most concerned the media at the press briefing the previous day. In a letter to Cadbury, who had missed the launch because of the death of his wife, Dearing noted the issues as:

(1) that our recommendations do not have enough clout behind them and that legislation would have been better;

(2) we have not done enough to bring the pay of executive board members under a strong framework of control and accountability to shareholders.

I think we gave good answers on both points, but you know what it is: a paper has a long established view and unless it is getting what it has long advocated, it will not be satisfied. This morning's press—especially the *Telegraph*—bears that out and I only wish I had been more successful in persuading them. The *Standard*, *The Times* and *Accountancy Age* are all good but I was sorry that we got such faint praise from the *Independent*

---

[2] CAD 03109.

and the *Financial Times*, whilst not all bad (except Lex), attributed two remarks to me that cause surprise—at least to me.[3]

First Reactions

In the *Financial Times*, there was a factual summary of the report's recommendations as well as a piece by Richard Waters, the latter identifying two assumptions underpinning the Cadbury proposals: the first was that self-regulation offered the best way forward and the second that the financial markets would impose tough sanctions on companies that did not put in place the accepted standards of corporate governance. Neither company compliance nor more active interest from shareholders could, he noted, be taken for granted. More critical was the Lex column in the same paper, questioning the letter rather than the spirit of the proposed Code, as well as suggesting that 'the great and the good who compiled it [the Code] do not wish to be inconvenienced by too much change'.[4] In fact, as we now know, it was not so much the compilers of the Report, but rather those who were going to implement it, who were averse to 'too much change'.

On the day after the launch Cadbury himself wrote in *The Times*, suggesting that only by improving the standards of corporate reporting and conduct could legislative

[3] CAD 01289.
[4] *Financial Times*, 28 May 1992.
[5] *The Times*, 28 May 1992.

regulation be avoided.[5] This was a point taken up and stressed in the paper's leading editorial in the same issue, where it referred to the Report as the 'last chance saloon' for self-regulation, a catchy phrase that was to recur in press comment.[6] The editorial went on to consider the Committee's purpose, as many others were to do in the next few weeks. Many and varied interpretations were suggested, not all bearing a close relationship to the Committee's terms of reference, set out in an appendix to the draft Report. *The Times* took an exceptionally narrow view of the Committee's objective, characterizing it as 'a report on how to stop fraud [which] is being described as on "the financial aspects of corporate governance"'. Going on to focus particularly on audit, to which it ascribed a more astringent function as the 'preventive self-medication of capitalism', rather than the current 'cosy' relationship obtaining between auditors and their corporate clients, the leader argued robustly that the Cadbury proposals must be 'ruthlessly and courageously administered'; only tighter self-regulation would stave off legislation. There was, however, little or no evidence that this was the case, at least nationally.[7] In a DTI press release on 10 June, timed to coincide with the CBI conference (see below), Neil Hamilton, Corporate Affairs Minister in

[6] A similar view was put forward by Tim Smith, an accountant and MP for Beaconsfield, in *Accountancy Age* on 4 June 1992.

[7] *The Times* leader did mention 'Brussels hovering'. By that it meant the proposed EU Fifth Company Law Directive. Chris Osman (of the City law firm Clifford Chance) noted: 'The Government has indicated that poor take-up of the Code may lead to regulations—indeed the proposed EC Fifth Company Law Directive may force its hand before then' (Osman 1992).

the Conservative administration that the April election had—unexpectedly—returned to power, emphasized the government's view that a voluntary system, embodied in the Code, was the way forward.[8] From the Opposition benches there was a different view; the Shadow Secretary for Corporate Affairs, Mo Mowlam, was 'disappointed' that the Report did not suggest 'fundamental change', presumably on the lines of the then Labour Party policy, which she had submitted to the Committee during the pre-publication consultation.[9]

The Sunday broadsheets on 31 May brought two very different reactions to the publication of the draft Report. As in its sister daily paper, the heaviest (and not always well informed) criticism came in the *Sunday Times*, where the journalist John Cassidy described the Report as 'a typically British compromise: well-meaning, reasonable, intelligent and worthless...based on the age-old British myth that capitalists are mild-mannered animals capable of learning good behaviour if only they go to the right schools'. He ended with a call for 'the best proposals [from the Report to be] strengthened, enshrined in a new Companies Act and policed by a well-financed regulator. Self-regulation has become a bad joke. It should be abandoned.'[10] In sharp contrast, writing in the *Observer*, Neville Bain, as we have seen a keen supporter of the Committee's purpose, discussed how corporate boards

---

[8] DTI press release, 10 June 1992.
[9] *Financial Times*, 28 May 1992.
[10] *The Times*, 31 May 1992.

could and should improve governance in order to avoid failure. Corporate governance, he concluded, 'is more about commitment than compliance'.[11]

Emerging Themes

In the plethora of editorials, articles, and letters to the editor that appeared in the next few weeks, some consistent criticisms and areas of contention emerged. One was that the accountants had got off lightly: not untypical was Andrew Jack in the *Financial Times*, who suggested that accountants across the country would be relieved when they read what he described as the 'favourable' findings in the Cadbury Report.[12] There had been—and continued to be—much public discussion of how the accounts of companies that had failed, among them of course Polly Peck and Maxwell, could have been signed off as satisfactory by auditors shortly before their collapse revealed fraud. This led to a proposal made to the Committee, with other extensive comments on the draft Report,[13] by A. J. Merrett (formerly Professor of Finance at the London Business School) and Allen Sykes, who had been CEO of Consolidated Goldfields. Their suggestion was that a new structure should be set up, with the

[11] *Observer*, 31 May 1992.
[12] *Financial Times*, 4 June 1992, in an article entitled 'Auditors Applaud as the Boat Remains Unrocked'.
[13] CAD 02141.

responsibility for appointing, remunerating, and direct-
ing auditors transferred from the shareholders to independent trustees, appointed by lenders and creditors.
This would, they argued, enable fraud to be detected at
an early stage. Perhaps because of the widespread criticism of auditors and of the way the draft Report had
dealt with them, the proposal was treated seriously by
Cadbury, who met Merrett and Sykes for discussions, and
their paper was sent to Committee members for comment.[14] It did not, however, stay the course for consideration at the Committee's meetings in the autumn, not
least because, as Charkham pointed out, 'their system
calls for two classes of director and in effect a formal
supervisory system which is three-quarters of the way
to a two-tier board'.[15] The prospect of a two-tier system
was regarded by both the CBI and IoD with hostility and
was, as we shall see, fundamental to their critiques of the
draft's monitoring proposals, so it is hardly surprising
that no more was heard of the Merrett–Sykes proposal.

There was also a good deal of questioning of how the
implementation of recommendations was to be enforced.
Writing in *The Times*, Robert Bruce, associate editor of
Accountancy Age, suggested that most of the Report was
'words which have no definite sanction behind them'.[16]
Burson–Marsteller, a public relations firm, carried out
a survey with twenty-two leading fund managers and

---

[14] CAD 02185.
[15] CAD 01073.
[16] *The Times*, 4 June 1992.

auditors in June. Among its findings—broadly that most of those questioned considered that the draft report's recommendations did not go far enough—was the particular concern about enforcement, with one institutional shareholder quoted as saying: 'There is no way of effective enforcement other than delisting at the Stock Exchange. That would be like using a nuclear weapon—in other words, it will never be used.'[17]

Another much discussed part of the Report was the role to be played in the governance process by the non-executive directors; it led to questioning of their availability, in both quantity and quality, to carry out the functions allocated to them. As Robert Bruce noted, 'the idea of an army of independent non-executive directors, all tough as old boots and as fair-minded as umpires, rising up to serve the corporate nation is another unlikely assumption'.[18] One highly critical review of the Report came, as the Committee no doubt expected, from Sir Owen Green, whose hostility to the Committee's work has already been noted. Characterizing the Report as 'long on accountability but short on drive and efficiency', in a Personal View column in the *Financial Times*, Green argued that, not only would the report's recommendations result in more bureaucracy and committees, but also that they were striking 'at the heart of the unitary board' by the powers to be entrusted to non-executive

[17] *Financial Times*, 11 June 1992.
[18] *The Times*, 4 June 1992.

directors to monitor performance.[19] These were all concerns and reservations that were to be reiterated in different degrees—if in less colourful language—in the many responses from companies, accountants, shareholders, and institutions, which started arriving at the Committee's secretariat in June and July. At the same time, Cadbury had a round of meetings and discussions to get a sense of the criticisms. For example, on 8 June he met the Stock Exchange Listing Advisory Committee, some of whose members were unhappy with responsibilities thrust upon the non-executive directors, more particularly with the proposal in the draft Report that non-executives should have 'an appointed leader'.[20]

Few, if indeed any, of the many pieces written about the Report and its proposals identified or acknowledged the difficulties that faced the Committee. These included its rather narrow remit (criticized by a number of journalists) and the need to create a consensus on an acceptable approach among the parties most directly involved; they, as noted in the previous chapter, held widely divergent views and, in some cases, prejudices. An editorial in *The Economist*, however, did suggest there were 'deeper roots' underpinning the establishment of the Committee, beyond the collapses of recently audited firms and the large rises in executive pay. These were the fears, to be found 'on both sides of the Atlantic, that the absence of committed owners is sapping corporate

---

[19] *Financial Times*, 9 June 1992.
[20] CAD 01155, Cadbury's notes on the meeting.

performance'. Describing the Cadbury recommendations as 'exceptionable only in their mildness', the editorial concluded: 'corporate governance is doomed to remain a messy compromise. Decades of modern capitalism have yielded no perfect model, nor will decades more.'[21] Early in June Peace began to prepare for the revision of the draft Report, first summarizing the initial critical press reactions.[22]

The Committee Fights Back

Two significant conferences were held in June, and at both members of the Committee mounted a strong defence of the proposals set out in the draft Report against the criticisms being levelled by the press and others. The first of these events was sponsored by the CBI (with the public relations consultants Burson–Marsteller); it was entitled 'Corporate Governance: Whose Business is it Anyway?' and took place on 10 and 11 June.[23] Three members of the Committee set out to counter some of the views so freely expressed in the press over the previous two weeks. On the morning of the first day, Sir Adrian Cadbury spoke, setting out the features of the Report, its recommendations, and the Code of Best Practice. He responded to the position of the CBI on the draft Report with a forceful warning: 'The recommendations on our draft report are aimed directly at

[21] *The Economist*, 30 May 1992.
[22] CAD 01291.
[23] CAD 02213.

raising the level of confidence in the way companies are run. If we do not take the initiative ourselves in this matter, others who understand business less well and are more doctrinaire in their approach will surely do so.'[24]

A comment he made in the course of his presentation, that the days of multiple non-executive directorships were over, was misinterpreted by some journalists, causing something of a storm in a teacup. Although the draft Report made no suggestion as to how many non-executive positions an individual might hold in 'best practice', Cadbury's comment led to speculation in the press that the revised Report and Code would recommend that non-executive directors should hold no more than one boardroom position at a time. A good deal of column space was spent on this over the next few weeks, until, in an address to a seminar sponsored by the Institute of Chartered Secretaries and Administrators, Cadbury made it clear that he had not meant to imply that it was advisable to hold only one such directorship. The 'multiple' directorships—according to the *Director* magazine some held up to ten non-executive posts—would not be possible with the increased role and responsibilities recommended for non-executives under the Code. But, as Cadbury went on to say: 'There are advantages in holding more than one outside directorship in terms of the exchange of experience and of making the best of scarce resources.'[25]

[24] Unnumbered paper.
[25] See *Guardian*, 16 July 1992, and *Financial Times*, 17 July 1992. See also CAD 02459, Peace letter to Association of Independent Museums, 4 August 1992.

To return to the CBI conference, later in the morning Cadbury was followed by Mike Sandland, chairman of the ISC and Committee member, whose presentation explored the role and influence of the institutional shareholder. Sandland began by referring to the 'substantial volume' of press comment, singling out the Cassidy article in the *Sunday Times*, with its characterization of the Report as 'worthless'; his purpose, he said, was to explain how far from worthless the Report was: 'Indeed, by enlisting the influential support of the investing institutions, I think it could well be a very significant step forward in the pursuit of higher standards of business behaviour.' Sandland outlined the development of the ISC, gave his personal endorsement to the Report, and, with the proviso that he had not as yet formally discussed it with ISC members, suggested that the ISC would also endorse it. Finally, to counter the criticism that the voluntary nature of the Code meant that it had no teeth, he suggested that the requirement for a statement of compliance or reasons for non-compliance, which would be a continuing listing obligation of the Stock Exchange, *did* provide the shareholders, whether institutional or individual, with teeth—or, as he put it, an opportunity for biting.[26]

The role of the Stock Exchange was the subject addressed by the Exchange's chairman, Andrew Hugh Smith, in his presentation. He began and ended by

[26] CAD 02213, CBI conference paper.

stressing that the Code did not contain any shocks, nor should it have done, since it was intended to 'encompass best practice, not some theoretical vision'. He went on to clarify the Stock Exchange 'involvement'—what was to become the 'comply or explain' part of the Code. This is worth quoting in full, given the misinterpretations that became common as to how this would work:

It is proposed that production of this statement be a continuing obligation of listing. The Committee is not proposing that every listed company complies with every aspect of the Code. There will be those for whom certain requirements are inappropriate. The Exchange is not going to monitor arrangements for corporate governance. It is not offering sanctions and punishment. It is going to require that that companies report their level of compliance so that divergence from the Code of Best Practice is revealed and an opportunity for explanation is given. The Exchange will disclose publicly details of companies which have significantly failed to comply. So compliance with the Code does not become a continuing obligation but shareholders will see clearly which companies have failed to comply with the Code.[27]

Hugh Smith concluded his presentation with a reiteration that the Code was not breaking new ground, nor was the Committee pursuing an unattainable Holy Grail (the phrase used in the *Guardian* of the Committee's objective). Rather: 'We are working with the spirit of the times.'

---

[27] Andrew Hugh Smith, 'The Role of Market Regulation in Corporate Governance', CAD 02213, CBI conference paper.

This, too, was the burden of the message contained in the speech delivered by the Governor of the Bank of England, Robin Leigh-Pemberton, to the conference.[28] While not a formal sponsor of the Committee, the Bank had given informal assistance, and the Governor expressed the Bank's approval of the Report, while noting its chief interest was in financial reporting and non-executive directors (as a supporter of PRO NED), and it was pleased to see the debate on corporate governance 'being carried forward with so much vigour'. He warned of the dangers of complacency, particularly when times were prosperous, going on to say: 'It is not that the United Kingdom lacks some of the best-run companies in the world but that there is such a wide spectrum from the best to the worst that the best seem not to realise how important it is to raise standards generally.' His response to the critics, 'those who question the general thrust of the recommendations', was a challenge: 'however well they themselves run their own companies, it must be said that the onus is on them to suggest better solutions'.[29]

The CBI conference was well covered by the press, as also was the second event, the ICAEW's annual conference held at Eastbourne on 25–27 June. Entitled 'Corporate Governance—a Time for Change', the draft Report once again was top of the agenda.[30] A keynote speech came from Mick Newmarch, since 1990 CEO of

[28] CAD 03109.
[29] CAD 03109.
[30] According to *Independent*, 23 June 1992.

the Prudential Group.[31] He began with a reprise of the long history of the Prudential (and his own part in it latterly) in pushing forward the corporate governance debate in the interests of protecting shareholders. He noted past occasions when the Prudential had stepped in, including the case of Horatio Bottomley (before his time) as well that of the Dockers and the BSA company (in 1956, just after he had joined the company).[32] Having established his own and the company's credentials, he moved on to some criticisms of the draft Report. These were, firstly, that the tone of the Report seemed to be too ready to assume that executive directors were the enemies of corporate governance, which was not the case in his experience; secondly, he argued that institutional investors should not go beyond protecting shareholders' interests; on audit he was opposed to the proposal to introduce compulsory rotation of audit firms and the introduction of audits for interim accounts; finally, while his support for non-executive directors was longstanding

---

[31] Mick Newmarch joined the Pru from school and was its chief investment manager through the 1980s. He died in 2010. See obituaries, *Daily Telegraph* and *Guardian*, 12 April 2010.

[32] For Horatio Bottomley, MP, journalist, and 'swindler', see A. J. A. Morris, 'Bottomley, Horatio William (1860–1933)', in *Oxford Dictionary of National Biography* (Oxford University Press, 2004) <http://www.oxforddnb.com/view/article/33757> (accessed 16 June 2012); for the Dockers and BSA (he was chairman and managing director of BSA from 1944 to 1956, when he was dismissed after a lengthy boardroom battle), see Richard Davenport-Hines, 'Docker, Sir Bernard Dudley Frank (1896–1978)', in *Oxford Dictionary of National Biography* (Oxford University Press, 2004); online edn, September 2010 <http://www.oxforddnb.com/view/article/46884> (accessed 16 June 2012).

and undimmed, he had concerns about there being a sufficient number with the independence and the experience to do the job well.[33] His conclusion, if not the most ringing of endorsements, at least argued for more action and less talk. The Cadbury Report, he said, albeit without anything 'startlingly new', 'provides a useful fresh impetus... What we need now is action to put good corporate governance in place at a much faster rate than has been happening so far.'[34]

Other speakers at the conference included Brandon Gough, chairman of Coopers & Lybrand, who concluded his analysis of what was wrong with audit (a failure to recognize significant changes in the environment in which auditors worked) with a call for reform: 'Cadbury has given us the opportunity to respond and to re-establish the prestige of audit'.[35] A note from Peace, who was attending the conference, suggested the speech had not gone well with a representative attending from KPMG.[36] As one press account of the conference suggested, with half of the ICAEW's members in public practice and the other half working in industry and commerce, while they would agree on the 'fundamentals', they were less likely to do so on the specifics.[37] We have already noted that the accountancy profession did not always speak with one voice, and this was to

---

[33] CAD 03225, Newmarch speech.
[34] CAD 03225, Newmarch speech. See also *Financial Times*, 27 June 1992.
[35] CAD 03110.
[36] CAD 03110.
[37] *Independent*, 23 June 1992.

be clearly demonstrated in the responses to the draft Report that were submitted to the Committee.

In his speech at Eastbourne, Newmarch had said, while discussing the role of non-executive directors:

We are at last seeing signs that non-executive teams are prepared to flex their muscles and take action. We may have seen it recently at Barclays and at NatWest. We saw it several times in 1990 and in 1991. We saw it, famously, at Guinness in the late 1980s. But in my view, it still does not happen often enough or quickly enough.

Hardly were the words out of his mouth when it was learned that, at BP, a boardroom coup, led by the non-executive directors, had ousted Robert Horton from the joint position he held as its chairman and chief executive, not, according to the Report, because he held both positions, while Cadbury recommended they should be held separately, but because of a combination of weak corporate performance on his watch and his 'dominating' management style. A non-executive chairman, Lord Ashburton, and full-time chief executive, David Simon, were appointed.

The issue of splitting the two roles had arisen at the CBI conference earlier in the month, when Sir Allen Sheppard had been taken to task for holding both positions at Grand Metropolitan. He had replied that 'he asked Sir John Harvey Jones to be chairman but he did not have the time so Sir John became a non-executive director and...Sir Allen assumed both roles'. He had gone on to say: 'We made sure there were plenty of checks and balances, but I agree that the roles should ideally be split.'[38] Another company that did not separate the roles of chairman and chief executive was Marks and Spencer. On 15 July 1992, Jonathan Charkham met Richard Greenbury of Marks and Spencer, who was later to play an important role in developing proposals on the contentious area of directors' remuneration, which, as we have noted, was largely beyond the Cadbury Committee's remit. Charkham's note of this meeting indicates that Greenbury was far from impressed by the draft Report and thought it contained 'an implicit assumption that the world was full of villains that needed taming'.[39] Greenbury was not the only industrialist to make that point.[40] He was also unhappy that the Report suggested that non-executives should become too involved in the business and he thought that an 'appointed' leader of the non-executives, as the draft Report suggested, would lead to a divided board. He observed that M&S already complied with most of the recommendations and that he would be explaining the company's approach to the combination of chairman and chief executive role and adding non-executives to the audit committee. Charkham noted: 'I explained to him the background to the Committee's thinking on these issues and I hope I left him feeling less reproachful towards them. As is so often the case, he needed

---

[38] *The Times*, 11 June 1992.
[39] CAD 01281.
[40] See, e.g., Corrin (1993), quoted in Chapter 5.

reminding that the high ethical standards and good management practices of his group were not unfortunately universal among the 2000 PLCs.'[41]

Through June and July, there were events in the corporate world that kept the issues raised by the draft Report, and relevant in one way or another to corporate governance, alive and in the headlines. Early in July a report from the Monks Partnership, UK Board Earnings, found that only seven companies in the FTSE 100 complied with the guidelines suggested by the draft Report on the remuneration of directors.[42] Towards the end of the month a survey commissioned by the London Stock Exchange and PRO NED into the role of the non-executive director was published. Sending a summary of these to Peace, Dearing highlighted the findings that 84 per cent of the institutional investors and auditors agreed that non-executive directors have a responsibility as a shareholders' watchdog; however, only 3 per cent of them agreed that non-executives were effective. Dearing went on to say:

That suggests that the institutional shareholders, who are very largely the owners of British Industry, do want the non-executives to have a distinctive and strong role on boards in the financial aspects of corporate governance, and that we must therefore resist being knocked off our perch by people like the CBI, who do not speak for the shareholders. As I have previously indicated, however, there are ways in which we can

[41] CAD 01281.
[42] *The Times*, 2 July 1992.

respond to the CBI concerns that we have unwittingly seemed to polarise the board into non-executives and executives.[43]

In its report of the survey, *The Times* had a rather different spin, drawing attention to the low response rate to the survey and suggesting therefore that there was 'a silent majority' of company chairmen who would need to be 'dragged' into 'Cadbury's new world'. Moreover, 'effective change will still depend on the quality and commitment of non-executives. Only a third of them replied.'[44]

The Responses to the Committee

During June and July the responses to the draft Report had been flooding in to the Committee's office. In format they ranged from single-sheet letters to lengthy memoranda and they came from individuals as well as companies and organizations, most managing to submit by the deadline of 31 July, with a few stragglers arriving in early August. Among the latter was an unpleasant surprise in the shape of the accountancy firm Ernst & Young's six-page commentary, described by Cadbury when he first read it as a 'demolition job', although admitting that he 'understood their concern about being sued'.[45] ('Demolition job' was also the description used—approvingly—by Sir Ronald

---

[43] CAD 01273.
[44] *The Times*, 30 July 1992.
[45] CAD 02447.

Grierson, in a letter to the *Financial Times*, commenting on Green's Personal View column in the paper.[46]) In
fact, while less than supportive, particularly in compari-
son with the responses of other accountancy firms,[47] the
response was not as destructive as it may have seemed on
first reading. Unlike many other respondents, who pref-
aced their criticism with an expression of support for the
'broad thrust' of the Report, Ernst & Young, with the brief-
est of nods in support of the Committee's 'aim', plunged
straight into detailing their doubts and misgivings. These
started with the Code, which generally seems to have been
less criticized than the draft Report itself, suggesting it was
'a combination of objective rules (regarding such matters
as the maximum duration of directors' service contracts)
and desired qualitative attributes of directors and boards
(such as the requirement for the board to retain full and
effective control over the company)'. However, they went
on to say that the Report was calling for actions to meet
'the spirit' of the Code, a view with which the Committee
would have agreed. While accepting some of the recommendations and criticizing others, Ernst & Young came
to the conclusion that it was doubtful whether self-regulation 'can provide the robust and responsive framework
necessary in today's business environment'. There were
others who shared that view. It is, however, worth noting that, two years later, M. J. Harding, who had been
much involved with the Ernst & Young response to the

---

[46] *Financial Times*, 10 June 1992.
[47] A partner in Ernst & Young, Nigel Macdonald, sat on the Committee.

draft Report, as well as the discussions at the CBI, wrote to Cadbury saying: 'in my experience...the Cadbury Report has been properly received and serious efforts have been made to comply with its recommendations. Perhaps, therefore, we were wrong, to a degree at least, in the concerns I expressed, since, so far, I would say that the realisation of the importance of proper corporate governance has been significantly enhanced.'[48]

There was, then, a formidable task facing the Committee, in considering so many and such varied views, suggestions, and comments, not only balancing them according to merit and acceptability, but also taking into account their source and its standing.[49] To prepare for the revision meetings scheduled for the autumn, Peace embarked in August on an extensive analysis of the responses, including all those received by the 14th of that month. Of the 209 consultation responses received by that date, 117 were categorized as 'generally supportive', 20 as 'not generally supportive', and 72 he placed as 'cannot be categorised'. Most of the respondents, he noted, had expressed reservations (in some cases substantial) about particular aspects of the Report.[50] He went on to analyse them further by their source, companies,[51] shareholders,[52] and accountants.[53] In all there were

---

[48] CAD 02475.
[49] Cadbury mentioned this in his steering note.
[50] CFACG (92) 15, 20 August 1992. Additional papers.
[51] CAD 02255.
[52] CAD 02257.
[53] CAD 02259.

seventy companies who had responded, most of which had not been involved in the pre-publication consultations. Many of the letters were so similar in format that Peace was moved to write on a Post-it note to Cadbury (attached to the letter from IMI) that he wondered whether they were based on a CBI blueprint.[54] The extensive correspondence surviving includes a letter from the Institute of World Economy and International Relations in Moscow, requesting a copy of the draft Report. It moved Peace to note: 'I think we can fairly claim to be the report that really reaches the parts that other reports do not reach!'[55] There was also a fourth (and smaller) category of responses that included consultants, academics, and lawyers. Within each category Peace highlighted the points made, quoted extracts, and noted criticisms, supportive statements, and suggestions made.

The Revisions

The Committee reassembled at the Bank of England on 17 September at 9.30 a.m. for a meeting scheduled to last until 5.30 p.m. (lunch would be provided, according to Peace's note to members). To the members, all present except Hugh Collum,[56] six papers had been previously circulated. These were a steering note by the chairman, and

[54] CAD 02123.
[55] CAD 02166.
[56] Sir Christopher Hogg, who had acted as an adviser to the Committee for the preparation of the draft Report and Code, was also present.

five notes drafted by Peace: his summary of the responses to the draft Report, together with notes on the publication of the Code as a separate document, on directors' remuneration, on the role of the company secretary, and on the role of the internal auditor.[57] Additionally a submission from the Hundred Group of Finance Directors (which had arrived only in early September) was sent out just before the meeting.

Cadbury's steering note, based on the overview of the responses to the draft Report, began by noting the question of how the Committee should deal with the large number of submissions it had received, whose 'weight' alone posed a number of problems. He went on to say:

To do it full justice would mean, in my view, re-considering our terms of reference and taking several more months over re-drafting. Cost and our reliance on Nigel Peace apart, this would not meet the expectations of those who are looking to the Committee for guidance and who are already (CBI letter) acting on our draft proposals. I suggest, therefore, that we should stick to our original timetable as best we can and simply address the key criticisms, while leaving the form and as far as possible the length of the Report as it is.

The timetable provided for three meetings, the last of which was to take place on 10 November, when the

---

[57] This was drafted by Peace as a result of several large companies urging that the final Report should emphasize more strongly the importance of an effective internal audit department. The Institute of Internal Auditors had submitted their comments in July, CAD 02419, and on 6 August a small deputation from the Institute presented their case to Cadbury in person.

final Report would be approved, so that it could be published on 1 December.[58] The procedure followed the pattern developed and used in drafting the Report: the long September meeting would discuss and decide on changes to be made, and these were to be embodied in an amended draft to be presented to the October meeting. The new draft would be considered at that meeting, along with any other areas where changes needed had not yet been made. These in turn would result in a completed redraft to be approved by the Committee at its final meeting in November.[59]

Cadbury went on to say that the Committee 'should consider acknowledging the extent and value of the comments which have been submitted and possibly add that they will form part of the input to our successor body'. Most significantly, he suggested that the Committee's approach to changes should be that 'there is no reason for us to make a change simply because of criticism [he noted that some criticisms cancelled each other out], but there are one or two points where all of us have probably had second thoughts and we need to build as much support as we can for those recommendations we regard as of prime importance'. The final background point he made, before going on to note specific issues, was

---

[58] Peace letter to committee members, 15 October 1992. Additional papers. Peace had a contingency plan 'if for any reason it is not possible to agree the final report at the meeting on 10 November and a further meeting is necessary, it will be held on the morning of 1 December instead of the press conference'. In the event it was not necessary.

[59] This process was not clearly articulated in the surviving papers but extrapolated from them by the authors. Additional papers.

that the Committee needed to be clear 'how queries on the implementation of our report are to be dealt with, between now and May 1994'.[60]

From Cadbury's steering note and the analysis, Peace had listed a table of points for discussion, numbering thirty-four in all, so the Committee had a good deal to get through at the day's meeting. While some of these items could be—and were—dealt with easily and the amendments quickly agreed, others, particularly in the areas where there were 'key criticisms', required a much lengthier discussion. To deal first with the former, the CBI and its members (as well as others responding) had suggested there should be a free-standing version of the Code printed to be made available to all companies and this was agreed. In fact it had probably been informally discussed and accepted before the meeting, since Peace was negotiating publication terms, including a free-standing version of the Code early in September.[61] There was some rewording to be done to reflect the changes in the body of the draft Report and the cross references in the draft Code to the relevant sections of the Report had to be deleted for the free-standing version.

As the chairman had suggested, further clarification of what would happen next was needed. The CBI, while noting that some of its members had already embarked on applying the Code, had urged a later date for compliance

---

[60] May 1994 was the date set for the winding-up of the Committee. Additional papers.

[61] Additional papers.

than that in the draft Report. The Committee responded to this by moving the date on a year. More specific provision was also necessary both for the immediate future and, in the longer term, for the successor body. It was agreed that Peace should discuss with the current sponsors the potential for that body to have wider terms of reference, which implied wider sponsorship—the CBI was suggested—but doubted whether the details could be arranged before the publication of the final Report.[62] More immediately, the Committee would continue under Cadbury's chairmanship, meeting perhaps every three months, but would require administrative support for the four tasks the chairman and secretary envisaged must be carried out. These were:

firstly to respond to enquiries, for example on interpreting the Code: secondly to keep track of developments, including publication of compliance statements by companies: thirdly to undertake preparatory work for the successor body's review, drawing on *inter alia* the submissions received: fourthly, liaison with the steering group of the ICAEW's Research Board which had agreed to fund research on corporate governance issues over the next two years.[63]

For the Report itself, the Committee agreed that a new introductory preface by the chairman should be added, with a reminder of the Committee's purpose, making 'the point firmly' that the Committee had addressed only

---

[62] Peace's minutes of September meeting. Additional papers.
[63] Peace letter, 22 September 1992. Additional papers.

the financial aspects of corporate governance. This was a response to the many different interpretations that, as we have seen, had been bandied about. In the first section of the Report the Committee turned its attention to the phrase in paragraph 1.7 of the draft Report: 'Had such a code been in existence in the past, we believe that a number of the recent examples of unexpected company failures and cases of fraud would have received attention earlier *and might have been avoided.*'[64] This had attracted considerable and largely unfavourable, sometimes even mocking, press comment; a more serious objection (mentioned in his note by Cadbury) had come from Michael Mumford, an academic at Lancaster University. He had argued that the proposals, albeit well intentioned,

do not constitute enforceable standards: I find it impossible to imagine Robert Maxwell, for example, hesitating for a moment before signing a statement confirming that MCC and MGN complied in every respect with Cadbury's Code of Conduct— and, more seriously, it is hard to see how either his fellow directors or the companies' auditors could have obtained sufficient evidence to mount a credible challenge to any such statement.[65]

A number of other responses had made the point, both specifically in connection with Maxwell and more generally in relation to fraud, that the actions of determined 'fraudsters' or 'criminals' could not be prevented by a Code of Best Practice. The Committee did not hesitate

[64] Emphasis added.
[65] M. J. Mumford, A Personal Response to the Cadbury Report. Additional papers.

in deciding to delete the phrase 'and might have been avoided'. It also agreed to add a further sentence indicating—as many of the responses had suggested—that, without making corporate life well-nigh impossible, no measure could prevent those determined to act fraudulently from doing so.

The definition of corporate governance used at the beginning of the draft Report had also attracted attention. Sir Owen Green and others had argued that to define it as 'the system by which companies are run' was wrong: directors and managers 'run' companies, they declared. An alternative wording was discussed, and, following further informal exchanges between the meetings, the wording 'the system by which companies are directed and controlled' was approved in October.

The responses revealed a variety of views on compliance and its enforcement. The IoD, the CBI, and the Stock Exchange Listed Companies Advisory Committee all supported compliance statements but differed as to whether such a statement should be a continuing obligation of listing; this was opposed by the CBI.[66] The Committee's discussion focused on the responsibility of shareholders for taking up with companies issues disclosed by compliance statements with which they were unhappy. It was emphasized that the Committee saw this as market regulation, rather than self-regulation, and, with the decision that a sentence should be added to acknowledge the important role of the press and analysts, no further

---

[66] CAD 02255.

amendment was necessary.[67] Similarly, although the Committee had received many representations on the difficulties and the costs of the application of the Code to small companies, particularly in terms of the need to appoint additional non-executive directors, it decided against any major change. The secretary recorded that the majority of the Committee was 'not disposed to make significant concessions in respect of small companies' and any acknowledgement of the difficulties should be 'carefully drafted so as not to provide a general escape route'.[68] On two proposals concerning directors—that all of them should be re-elected every three years and that best practice on service contracts was three years' fixed or one year's rolling—the Committee had 'mixed views', as noted by the secretary. Both of these, together with a proposal for greater disclosure on directors' pay, being arguably beyond the Committee's remit, were 'logged as a matter for the successor body'.[69]

The most complex areas of the draft and the Code, which had drawn the most critical and hostile responses, polarizing views inside and outside the Committee, were those covering the board of directors, non-executive directors, and the functions they were to carry out, such as their role on audit committees. At one end of the spectrum were the views encapsulated in the response of Sir Alick Rankin, chairman of Scottish & Newcastle plc, who

---

[67] Minutes of September meeting. Additional papers.
[68] Minutes of September meeting. Additional papers.
[69] Minutes of September meeting. Additional papers.

wrote: 'The code, as proposed, appears to identify non-executives as the "gamekeepers" and executives as "the poachers."'[70] But the role of non-executive directors as 'monitors' or 'watchdogs', the latter term frequently employed by respondents, was widely contested. That role, and more particularly the proposal in the Report that non-executives should have 'an appointed leader' to deal with the rest of the board, had been interpreted as one that divided the board, leading ultimately to a two-tier structure, the prospect of which was anathema to many—although not all—at that time. The threat to the unitary board, as it was seen, united the more severe critics such as Green and many of more moderate views in the CBI, which was implacably opposed to a two-tier structure. Some explanation of this was offered by Cadbury himself in a paper he wrote in early September:

A number of responses to the Committee's proposals have expressed concern that strengthening the position of non-executive directors on boards and giving them in some degree a monitoring role, based on their standing further back from the day-to-day management of the business than the executives, would divide the board. In effect, they argue, the committee's recommendations could mark a step towards a two-tier board in all but name, but without the clearly defined and separate responsibilities for supervision and management which the two-tier board enforces... While I do not share this concern that the Committee's proposals will covertly lead to two-tier boards, it prompts the question, why should the two-tier

---

[70] CAD 02455.

board model be so vehemently opposed by those who speak for British industry? I am a member of a supervisory board myself and I suspect that much of the opposition to two-tier boards in this country stems from the Bullock Committee and its advocacy of so-called worker directors.[71]

The secretary's minutes record succinctly—after what was undoubtedly a long discussion—that 'the Committee's support for the unitary board to be affirmed in 1.6 [in the amended Report it was also affirmed elsewhere] although not in such a way as to rule out companies adopting features of a two-tier structure if they want, or to prejudice future debate'.[72] It was also agreed that the wording of the proposal that non-executives should have an appointed leader should be reconsidered. Dearing had proposed an amendment, but the discussion at the September meeting was 'inconclusive'; further amendments were made, and in the final Report the 'appointed leader' disappeared. In the process of revision, other changes were made to the 'monitoring' role of the non-executives: directors were to have the right to attend audit committees, although membership would remain exclusive to the non-executives.

All these changes, as well as some minor amendments to the section on auditing (some based on consultation with the Auditing Practices Board) and some rewording 'to dispel the view that the Committee takes a negative view of governance', were embodied in the new versions

---

[71] Additional papers.
[72] Additional papers.

of the Report and the Code, produced by the secretary and the chairman, with informal and frequent consultations with Committee members after the September meeting and presented to the Committee for consideration at the meeting on 7 October.

Shortly before the Committee's final pre-publication November meeting, Cadbury had a foretaste of some critical responses when he attended the CBI conference in Harrogate. At that event, Martin Taylor of Hanson, chairman of the CBI companies committee (and soon to become a member of the revamped Cadbury Committee), set out the CBI objections. Although the CBI supported the self-regulatory approach, the listing requirement was seen as making the Code less flexible and increasing bureaucracy, while enforcement through the sanction of delisting was viewed as unlikely to be effective. Cadbury's response was to emphasize the role of the market and the central importance of the statement of compliance in providing shareholders, rather than any regulatory body, with the basis for action. The CBI also acknowledged the important role of non-executive directors but feared that, in recommending specific functions for them, the Report would undermine the concept of the unitary board. Directors would be divided into what Peter Morgan, director-general of the Institute of Directors, described as 'the doers and the checkers'.[73] Cadbury responded that the

[73] Peter Martin, 'Taming the Overmighty Boss', *Financial Times*, 2 December 1992.

final Report would clarify the Committee's strong support for the unitary board principle.

The final version of the Report and Code was approved at the November meeting and published on 1 December 1992.

5

Launching the Final Report: The Devil is in the Detail

The final Report and Code of Best Practice were published on 1 December 1992. On that date a letter was sent to all the chairmen of companies quoted on the London Stock Exchange, enclosing three copies of the Report and Code. The letter stated that the Code was voluntary but that, under the continuing obligations of listing on the Stock Exchange, companies would be required to state whether they were complying with the Code and to provide reasons for any non-compliance.[1] It was emphasized that the continuing obligation rules did not require actual compliance: the role of the Stock Exchange was to ensure that shareholders received the necessary information about governance arrangements and it was up to shareholders to pursue any issues arising that indicated that

---

[1] There is no mention here of the phrase 'comply or explain', which later came into use as a convenient summary of this requirement.

companies were not in compliance with the Code. The letter also advised that the Committee would 'remain in existence to act as a source of authority on the Code and its other recommendations. A new Committee will be set up by the end of June 1995 to take stock of progress and examine whether the Code needs updating.'[2]

On the same day, a press conference was held in the Barber-Surgeon's Hall in the City of London. One commentator noted an interesting juxtaposition: the large Holbein painting of the power-hungry Henry VIII incorporating the barbers and the surgeons into the livery company in 1540, hanging behind the members of the Committee who were 'preaching the message of greater power-sharing in corporate boardrooms'.[3] All the members of the Committee attended, together with representatives of the sponsors. Preparations for this event were made in a similar way to those for the draft Report: Peace's briefing notes[4] attempted to anticipate criticism and Cadbury made extensive notes linking the issues raised in the consultation on the draft Report with the changes made in the final version.[5] From these notes Peace constructed an opening statement, which Cadbury then amended.[6] The statement emphasized the role of disclosure and pointed out, as in the letter to chairmen,

---

[2] CAD 01345.

[3] Andrew Jack, 'Report Sets Out an Ambitious Remit for Self-Regulation', *Financial Times*, 2 December 1992.

[4] CAD 01311.

[5] CAD 01313.

[6] CAD 01315.

that it was not compliance with the Code that was enforced by the Listing Rules but the provision of a statement of compliance.[7] It went on to elaborate how the final Report clarified various issues raised by commentators on the draft Report but made it very clear that these were not major changes to the recommendations. The statement concluded by noting the inclusion in the Report of a reference to the role of the media 'in drawing attention to governance issues of public or shareholder concern'.

An examination of twenty-one press reports[8] relating to the Committee published between 26 November and 5 December 1992 provides an indication of the response to the publication of the final Report and Code. Most of the criticisms had already been voiced in comments on the draft Report and were predictable, given the constituencies expressing them.[9] Positive support for the Committee's work was almost universal, but some commentators suggested that this was superficial. Even the most vociferous critics managed to produce some grudging support, including the CBI, who expressed the view that a code would be more easily updated than

---

[7] Oddly, Cadbury's statement did not mention the associated explanation of any non-compliance.

[8] From the *Guardian*, *The Times*, the *Financial Times*, *The Economist*, and the *Independent*.

[9] Some headline writers could not resist the temptation of the confectionery theme: 'Soft Centre to Cadbury's Proposals' (*Independent*, 2 December 1992); 'Hard Centre Cadbury' (*Guardian*, 2 December 1992). A legal scholar also observed: 'One might conclude (having avoided metaphor thus far) that it is on the particular issue of self-regulation that the Committee was wrong to place all its creme eggs in one basket' (Finch 1992).

the law, and the Institute of Directors,[10] who acknowledged the 'tempering' of the recommendations regarding non-executive directors, recommendations that they had seen as undermining the unitary board principle. Although the role of non-executive directors did seem to have been slightly reduced from the draft proposals, concerns remained about the available pool of potential non-executives and about their quality and ability to fulfil their anticipated role.[11] Enforcement was viewed as a major concern. Concerns expressed at the launch of the draft Report were reiterated, especially with regard to whether the Code could have deterred Maxwell.[12]

Criticism was also raised by the accountancy firm Ernst & Young, which, as noted in Chapter 4, had in August 1992 submitted a lengthy comment on the draft Report, arguing that self-regulation was unlikely to raise corporate governance standards.[13] In response to these views, Cadbury repeated his earlier warning to the CBI, noted in Chapter 4: 'If we do not take the initiative in this matter, others who understand business less well and are more doctrinaire in their approach will surely do so.'[14] Those arguing that the Committee should have

[10] Richard Waters, Michael Cassell, and Andrew Jack, 'Reservations Underlie Welcome for Cadbury', *Financial Times*, 2 December 1992.
[11] Graham Searjeant, 'Making the Cadbury Code Work Will Test City's Mood for Change', *The Times*, 2 December 1992.
[12] 'Cadbury on Corporate Governance', *The Economist*, 5 December 1992.
[13] CAD 02447; Andrew Jack, 'Cadbury Faulted by Ernst & Young', *Financial Times*, 4 November 1992.
[14] Larry Elliott, 'Cadbury Says Fraud Risk Must Be Cut to Avoid Controls', *Guardian*, 11 November 1992.

recommended stronger enforcement arrangements did not provide any clear ideas as to how these might be designed, apart from one suggestion for a formal regulatory body similar to the City Panel on Takeovers and Mergers. This was apparently given short shrift by Cadbury.[15] The promise of review by a successor committee was seen by some commentators as a 'veiled threat': *The Economist* described this sentence in the Report as a dark hint and suggested that it might be insufficient to enforce compliance.[16]

There were some congratulatory messages, from Robin Leigh-Pemberton at the Bank of England,[17] from David Tweedie at the Accounting Standards Board,[18] from US corporate governance commentator Martin Lipton,[19] and from former US Securities and Exchange Commission commissioner A. A. Sommer.[20] Cadbury also received a particularly warm letter from Viscount Watkinson, who had been a staunch supporter and from his own experience was well aware of the challenge Cadbury had faced:

What makes me very pleased is the general acceptance of the main thrust of the report. At a time when the media starts in angry and bitter fear at every passing shadow, this is no mean achievement on your part and gives the code the best possible

---

[15] Graham Searjeant, 'Staging Post on Road of Reform', *The Times*, 3 December 1992.

[16] 'Cadbury on Corporate Governance', *The Economist*, 5 December 1992.

[17] CAD 02497.

[18] CAD 02500.

[19] CAD 02508; see also Lipton and Lorsch (1992).

[20] CAD 02508.

start. I am sorry that the CBI has not been more helpful but I feel that they too are suffering the reaction to bad times affecting their members. So you have launched successfully against a sea of troubles that I am afraid shows little sign of abatement in the near future.[21]

Individual critics remained sceptical, particularly of the expected contribution of non-executive directors, echoing criticism of the draft Report noted in the previous chapter. John Corrin, then chief executive of Allied Textiles, wrote an article in *Accountancy* with the challenging title 'A Blatant Slur on Executive Directors' Integrity', in which he described the Report as being 'like a script for a "soap" where the non-executive director is cast as saint, the auditor is a tarnished guardian angel, and the executive director is a villain' (Corrin 1993).

The Constant Critic

Owen Green, a critic of the Committee from its inception, as noted in Chapters 2 and 4, continued to voice his concerns throughout the post-report period. On 24 February 1994, Green delivered the Pall Mall lecture to the Institute of Directors.[22] This reiterated his view that the concept of the unitary board had been undermined

---

[21] CAD 02501.
[22] CAD 02279.

by the Report: 'But the fading reality of a unitary board will be further diluted by continuing emphasis on the distinctive roles of non-executives in governance.' His views on the role of the non-executive director are not easy to unravel. He argued, incorrectly, that the legal liability of non-executive directors had increased and it would therefore be difficult to find suitable people to serve in this capacity. He stated: 'The role of Auditor should be strengthened and his independence forti-fied by adequate professional and commercial protec-tion. This will release the nonexecutive director from his Cadburian watchdog role and restore him to one of constructive contribution to a unitary board's activ-ities.' But it is not at all clear what such a contribution might be, since he did not believe that the board as a whole had much of a strategic role:

Board review and endorsement of strategy—yes. But the idea of non-executives making significant contributions to strategy is not very realistic. As an analogy one recalls the eminent contributions to the strategies of war made by von Clauswitz [sic], Liddle Hart, De Gaulle and Guderian, all men steeped in the technology of their subject. In contrast the contributions to strategy by Churchill and his cabinets and Hitler and his political posse have not been well-regarded by historians.

On 5 March 1995, the *In Business* programme on BBC Radio 4 was devoted to the question of 'Who's Bossing the Bosses?'. Peter Day, the host, interviewed a series of people with an interest in corporate governance, including both Cadbury and Green.[23] Both reflected on the effect that the Code and recommendations had had. Green remained very critical of the Cadbury view of the value of non-executive directors: 'one of the Cadbury proposals was and is that non-executive directors should be responsible for strategy. Well, I think that's crazy. My view is that the strategy is very much a part of the executive contribution to the company because who knows more than the man running the operation and involved in the marketplace.'[24] Green was apparently taken to task by Cadbury for this inaccurate representation of the proposals and responded with a letter of apology.'[25] In this letter he repeated his previously expressed views on the role of the non-executive director.

But I would wish to make the following further comments on this issue of strategy.

Your Draft Report of 27.5.92 made, I believe, a reference to non-executive directors bringing an independent judgement to bear on the issue of strategy.

Research conducted in July 1992 under the sponsorship of the LSE and PRO NED, included a 'key finding' that there was a divergence of views across audiences as to what form non-executive input should take. Chairmen and non-executive directors perceived the role as to *contribute to the development of strategy*.

---

[23] The other interviewees were Alan McDougall of PIRC; fund manager David Herro; Sir Nigel Mobbs, chairman of Slough Estates and a member of the successor committee; William Crist, president of CalPERS; and Sophie l'Helias of a French firm of investment advisers.

[24] From transcript of broadcast *In Business*, BBC Radio 4, 5 March 1995. Unnumbered paper, box 13.

[25] CAD 01375. Underlining is that of Green.

Other board members and (notably) the institutional shareholders and audit partners see the role to be to comment on strategy formulated by the executive members of the board.

Your Final Report of 1.12.92 stated, inter alia (with my underlines):

The Code of Best Practice 1.3...'The Board should include non-executive directors of sufficient calibre and *number* to carry significant weight...'

The Report Introduction 2.5...'The responsibilities of the board include *setting* the Company's strategic aims, providing the leadership to put them into effect.

Code Principles 3.5...'(The Code) will assist the board in *framing* and winning support for their strategies'.

Taking all these references together, the role of independent judges to which you refer may well be regarded by non-executives as inconsistent with the more creatively structural requirement of 2.5 and 3.5 above.

My Pall Mall lecture (extract included) last year set out my view of the overstatement in the Cadbury wording of the Board's role in setting and framing the strategic aims, as distinct from review and ultimate endorsement of those aims.

He then offered some grudging approval of the Report's impact, before identifying an issue for the successor body to address more closely, that of the chairman's role.

I was critical of your qualified recommendation as to the separation of the roles of Chairman and C.E.O. However your proposals do seem to have influenced companies to effect that vital distinction. More now needs to be considered about the Chairman's election.

...You may gather from this that, after retirement and reflection, I now believe the importance of the role of Chairman can hardly be over-emphasised in an age in which the concept of a free market has been so misunderstood and exploited and in which liberty has become licence at company board levels.[26]

Consolidating the Consensus: December 1992 to May 1995

Most committees producing reports launch their final output, engage in a period of public promotion of its message, and then disband, leaving the implementation of their recommendations to others. The Cadbury Committee set a different pattern. The original difficulty of setting the remit for the Committee's work made it clear from the outset that there were several issues that were unlikely to be resolved in the short term and that others might appear during the Committee's term of office, given the rapidly changing economic environment. The Committee was aiming to codify best practice, and the very notion of best practice embodies an implicit dynamic that responds to environmental change. The Committee included in its Report the stipulation that its work should be reviewed by a successor body, and it remained in place for a further three years after the Report and Code had been published.

---

[26] It seems unlikely that Cadbury would have disagreed with these sentiments, and indeed he published a book on this topic ten years later (Cadbury 2002).

Cadbury's involvement in this lengthy interim period was clearly a concern, as a note from Peace to Cadbury in July 1992 demonstrates. He was worried that, if Cadbury was 'too absent from the scene', there would be a lack of 'focused ownership' of the Report, damaging the credibility of the whole enterprise.[27] Cadbury agreed to remain as the 'recognised figurehead' until the review took place.

There were several changes after the Report had been published. The IoD and the CBI became additional sponsors (discussions were held with the ISC, which eventually declined). Nigel Peace handed over the secretarial role to Gina Cole, and the secretariat moved from ICAEW to an office at the Stock Exchange. Martin Taylor, vice chair of Hanson and chair of the CBI companies committee, replaced Ian Butler. Sarah Brown returned as DTI observer in September 1994 after she had taken over as Head of Companies Division at the DTI. Sir Sydney Lipworth, succeeding Dearing as chairman of the FRC, joined the Committee in February 1994, with Dearing stepping down to become an adviser to the Committee.[28] Committee meetings took place regularly throughout the period until the appointment of the successor committee in 1995. The Committee also

[27] Additional papers.

[28] In an update for Sydney Treadgold at the FRC, dated 18 October 1994, Gina Cole set out details of the financial support provided by sponsors for the period April 1993 to March 1994: £8,000 each from the IoD, the CBI, and the FRC, and £4,000 each from the 'Big 8' accountancy firms. The same sums were requested for the period April 1994 to May 1995. CAD 01341.

established a Monitoring Sub-Committee, intended to collect information about the adoption of the Code by companies to inform the deliberations of the successor group. The work of this group is discussed in more detail in the next chapter.

Responding to Queries

Queries began to arrive almost immediately after the final Report appeared. All queries about interpretation were dealt with in a constructive manner. Cadbury would often respond to the enquirer with an initial observation and the promise that the Committee would review the query with a more considered response to follow. In some cases, the enquirer would be told that the issue would be referred to the successor committee to keep under review. An example of such a response was sent to Alan Smallbone of the Pension and Population Research Institute on 16 March 1993:[29]

One of our objectives in keeping the committee in being until we hand over to our successors is to pick up points of difficulty which should be considered by those who will review the Code of Best Practice and its working. Equally, we are ready to clarify what we mean by any of our recommendations if there is doubt as to how they should be interpreted. I will make sure

---

[29] CAD 02267.

that the issue which you raise is on our agenda and I am grateful to you for pointing it out.[30]

The topics addressed at committee meetings can be
broadly classified into three areas: questions about interpretation of the Code and recommendations; issues
relating to compliance; and areas of concern which lay
beyond the Committee's remit. There was a continuing
need to emphasize the intention behind the statement
of compliance and associated explanation and to ensure
that the Committee's intention and ongoing activities
were accurately reported in the media.

The queries received suggest that some of those charged
with implementing the Code would have preferred more
concrete rules and there was a constant need to reiterate that this had not been the Committee's intention.
For example, to a query about directors' rolling contracts
raised by a company chairman, Cadbury had replied, as
usual, that it had not been the Committee's intention
to prescribe but to establish principles and guidelines.

---

[30] Most enquirers were satisfied with this process, but Smallbone apparently was not. He had argued that the use of the word 'contributions' in
paragraph 3.2 of the Code would allow full details of directors' pension
entitlements to be withheld. Cadbury replied to him that the word 'entitlements' might have been more appropriate than 'contributions' and that
he would raise this with the Committee. However, the Committee was
not minded to make any change to the wording at that time. Informed of
this, Smallbone took this correspondence to the press. Smallbone asserted
that Cadbury had changed his mind as a consequence of being 'nobbled'
and that this had resulted in 'cold, calculated fudge'. Cadbury responded
tartly that he had not been nobbled and commented: 'We can't rewrite
the report every five minutes. It's up to shareholders to institute enquiries
where they feel they are not getting enough information' (*Independent on
Sunday*, 11 July 1993).

Boards should disclose their policies on contracts so that shareholders could then take up any issues.

My main concern is that boards should sort these matters out for themselves and not look to the Committee for guidance which it is no position to give in any individual case.[31]

Concerns about the role of non-executive directors, first expressed in response to the draft Report, lingered. Gavin Burnett, a retired accountant who had played an active role in the profession in Scotland, wrote on 8 December 1992, reiterating a query he had raised in his response to the draft Report.[32] In his capacity as chair of an audit committee, he sought advice on the extent to which an audit committee could be responsible for reviewing the internal audit programme, given that its members are non-executive directors and lack inside knowledge of the company. In a draft response, Peace noted that it was 'not the Committee's intention that audit committees should involve themselves (unless they want to) in the nuts and bolts of internal audit investigations... our expectation is simply that the audit committee should generally understand and endorse the objectives of the internal auditors, their annual audit plan and their areas of emphasis'.[33]

In August 1993 the Institute of Investment Management and Research raised a query about the wording of the

---

[31] CAD 02269.

[32] CAD 02503.

[33] Expectations of the role of audit committees have extended quite dramatically in subsequent years.

Code in relation to the definition of executive and non-executive directors in the context of the role of the chairman, noting that chairmen were describing themselves in a variety of ways, with potential confusion for readers of company reports. This was discussed at the Committee meeting on 9 September where the view was agreed that it was for companies to decide on the appropriate terminology.

Correspondence with PIRC in 1995 raised an issue about how the independence of non-executive directors should be defined. PIRC had judged a company to be non-compliant with the Code, based on their judgement of independence, and the company in question had challenged this since this differed from the assessment of the company's board and paragraph 4.12 of the Report left this to the board to decide. Cadbury's view was that PIRC's criteria for judging independence went 'wider than any that I know of, either here or in the United States'[34] and he advised that, if their assessment of non-compliance was based on the issue of independence, they should make these criteria very clear, as others might interpret paragraph 4.12 differently. He noted with regret that the final sentence of paragraph 4.12—'Information about the relevant interests of directors should be disclosed in the Directors' Report'—did not form part of the Code, since such information was the basis for any judgement about independence. He included with his letter an extract

[34] CAD 02333.

from a talk he had given to the Institute of Advanced Legal Studies:

The Committee has set out a simple guideline and put the responsibility for applying it where it belongs. That is to say it is for boards to come to their own conclusions on the matter and to carry their shareholders with them. But if shareholders are to be in a position to judge how far directors are independent, they will need a fuller account of directors' interests that the contract-based declaration laid down by the Companies Act.

Small Companies

David Lewis of Molyneux Estates wrote on 2 December 1992,[35] noting the burden of compliance for the smaller company. Peace replied, noting that the Committee had recognized this in paragraph 3.15 of the Report and had anticipated that companies finding difficulty in complying initially would provide explanations for non-compliance, thus effectively complying with the Code provisions. He emphasized that the Committee also anticipated that compliance would benefit smaller companies, particularly in appointing non-executive directors.

The meeting in September 1993[36] addressed concerns that had been raised by the Association of Chartered

---

[35] CAD 02503.
[36] CAD 02269.

Certified Accountants (ACCA) and the City Group for Smaller Companies (CISCO) about the burden placed on smaller listed companies in complying with the Code, in terms of cost and administration. Cole's note for the meeting pointed out that 'the Committee did discuss the question of smaller companies prior to the publication of the Report and decided against any special provision for them'. The establishment of a different treatment would depend on finding a suitable definition of the small listed company, and there would be implications for assessing Code compliance if a company moved in or out of the category during the year. A more fundamental problem was the possibility of lobbying for relaxation of the Code from other groups, ultimately leading to 'total dilution'. The minutes recorded that Cadbury and Hugh Smith had met the head of CISCO: a face-to-face meeting was typical of Cadbury's approach to exploring issues raised. It was agreed that a watching brief would be kept on research being undertaken within the accountancy profession and that this could be an issue for the successor committee to pick up. Maintaining the integrity of the Code as a whole became a continuing preoccupation.

A written comment[37] from de Trafford emphasized that the IoD could see no good reason for smaller quoted companies to be exempt:

indeed, since many may be relative newcomers to the market they will have little track record of dealing with Stock Exchange obligations. It might be thought therefore that they should be

---

[37] CAD 02533.

expected to comply more strictly with the Code than those with a longer record.

Going Concern and Reporting on Internal Control

The two issues on which the Committee had recommended that the accountancy profession should develop guidance for those implementing the Code rumbled on for some time as debates within the profession continued among the various groups concerned.

At the November 1993 meeting[38] there was a lengthy discussion about the progress of the accountancy profession in producing guidance on going concern as requested in the Report (paragraph 5.22). The APB had produced draft guidance for auditors, and the ICAEW Working Party had produced draft guidance for directors, but a difference of opinion had arisen between the two groups as to the length of time into the future that the going concern statement should cover. The APB was planning to issue another exposure draft to invite further comment. Committee members were clear that it was not the role of the Committee to choose between the two approaches.

The minutes record that:

The Chairman considered that there was an issue of principle for the Committee, in that the Committee asked for guidance

---

[38] CAD 02271.

to be developed on certain issues in order that companies should know what was expected of them when complying with the Code of Best Practice. Understandably, when issues have been looked at they have become broader than the original recommendation in the Report. The question arises as to what extent it might be possible to split guidance being prepared into that part which relates to the specific issues raised by the Committee, and the wider issues arising...The second point of principle concerned the nature of the committee's authority. Recommendations are being made to the Committee for endorsement whereas the Chairman felt that this was not the Committee's job.

Taylor expressed concern that the proposed requirements could result in increased costs for companies. Sheldon and Sandland were concerned about maintaining the practicability of the Code. Cadbury subsequently wrote to the APB[39] clarifying the Committee's role with regard to the guidance. He noted that the Committee 'is not qualified to endorse accounting or auditing proposals, nor to publish them' and suggested that the form of guidance should share the characteristics of the Code— that is, it should be based on statements of principle, be brief, and be practicable, so that 'well-run companies' would not need 'to devote significant additional resources to compliance'. He also urged that guidance should be limited to the particular issues over which advice had been sought and suggested a proposed format for the guidance—a short statement of principles,

---

[39] CAD 02271, letter to Bill Morrison, APB, 9 December 1993.

addressing the specific issues, supported by a longer document 'covering related matters, plus working examples and other material'. The letter concluded with a reiteration of the need to preserve the balance on which the Code's authority rested:

The Committee's authority derives from the bodies which set it up and the perception by boards and their shareholders that its proposals strike a reasonable balance between costs and benefits. If that balance was not being seen to be held over any one of the Committee's recommendations, the support of the corporate sector for the rest of the Committee's recommendations could be at risk.

Maintaining this fragile consensus was an ongoing challenge for the committee.

In February 1994 the unresolved issues relating to going concern were again discussed.[40] De Trafford commented that the IoD was unhappy that the APB was attempting to define directors' duties: it was up to the board to make a judgement on going concern and the auditors to ensure that proper process had been undertaken in arriving at that judgement. 'The Chairman confirmed that the Committee should resist pressure to be drawn into the public debate. The Committee's role was to make the recommendation and for others to make decisions on implementation.' Guidance for auditors was finally issued in November 1994. The issues arising from Code paragraph 4.5—'The directors should report on the effectiveness

---

[40] CAD 02277.

of the company's system of internal control'—took far longer to resolve. The Internal Control Working Group was established to fulfil the requirements of the profession to develop guidance on internal control. The group was chaired by Paul Rutteman, a technical partner at Ernst & Young, and comprised individuals nominated by the Hundred Group of Finance Directors, ICAEW, and ICAS. At the May 1994 meeting[41] the main agenda item was a presentation by Rutteman, on the exposure draft on guidance that the working group had prepared, summarizing the responses received. To inform the discussion, Cole circulated a detailed summary of earlier comments made directly to the Committee on the issue.

The working group sought guidance from the Committee on several issues. Respondents to the exposure draft had argued that reporting on effectiveness was too onerous; there was concern that 'internal control' was wider than 'internal financial control'; some had commented on the lack of distinction between large and small listed companies; and the balance between principles and detailed guidance had also been questioned. However, it was clear from the working group's report that there was little agreement among the respondents as to how these issues might be dealt with.

There are no minutes of this meeting in the archive, but it is clear from the minutes of the September 1994 meeting[42] that much discussion had taken place both at

---

[41] CAD 02279.
[42] CAD 02293.

the May meeting and through subsequent correspondence. At the September meeting, a further discussion addressed how the Committee should respond to the revised draft of the guidance:

The Chairman said that in his view 'reporting on' the effectiveness of a system of internal control by directors would signify taking responsibility. He considered that the Committee had not intended directors to assume any additional burden, but had aimed to clarify existing responsibilities. The Committee itself does not have authority and there was a consequent need to preserve the general standing of the Code, and not place the Committee in an adversarial position *vis a vis* the profession.

It was eventually agreed that some endorsement of the proposed guidance was necessary. Two wordings were suggested, with Cadbury finally proposing that he would draft an endorsement for circulation and comment. Complete compliance with paragraph 4.5 was seen as an evolutionary process, and the successor committee would need to consider the issue.

The main item on the agenda for the December 1994 meeting was, once again, internal control, and Rutteman made a further presentation. He had written to Cadbury on 25 November[43] setting out the results of the consultation on the revised draft of guidance, which had received broad acceptance. As a result of the May discussions, the revised exposure draft had included: 'Directors may wish and are encouraged

---

[43] CAD 02299.

145

to state their opinion on the effectiveness of the system of internal financial control.' This had attracted a polarized set of responses, with a majority asking for the paragraph to be removed but others considering it very important and perhaps not strong enough. The majority of the working group believed it should be retained, while a minority wished to remove it. The working group agreed that the guidance should comply with the Code, so the issue was being presented to the Committee for further guidance.

All Committee members were present for this meeting, and the minutes report a constructive debate, centring mainly on the legal issues involved and concluding that 'the majority of the Committee were in favour of retaining the aim of reporting on effectiveness'. The working group was asked to provide a form of words that would leave it to boards to follow their own judgement but still encouraging expressions of opinion. It was confirmed that, whatever form of words was agreed, following the guidance would constitute compliance with the Code.[44] Cadbury then drafted a foreword to the proposed guidance[45] to this effect.

The final report from the group, 'Internal Control and Financial Reporting: Guidance for Directors of Listed Companies Registered in the UK', was published in December 1994, although the issue was not fully resolved until the guidance produced by the Turnbull

---

[44] CAD 02285; CAD 02317.
[45] CAD 02295.

working party was published in 1999.[46] This illustrates the way in which the Committee, led by its chairman, sought to respond constructively to demands to provide detailed guidance, while at the same time ensuring that it was not drawn into adopting a partisan stance where different groups did not agree. A central concern of the Committee was to preserve the integrity of the Code and to reiterate its intention that those involved should develop their own interpretations and implementations of the Code principles. While the chair's approach enabled a consensus to be reached among Committee members, no general consensus existed among auditors or preparers and the coordination of guidance was complex, with continuing difficulties about the authority of groups and the scope of their remit. The minutes of the February 1994[47] meeting note: 'The Committee's successor body would also need to consider carefully how any actions they proposed fitted into the whole jigsaw.'[48]

Further insights into the debate about internal control reporting are revealed in the minutes of the discussions of the informal 'overload' group. This had been established in response to concerns expressed about the impact on companies of compliance not only with the Code but with the avalanche of accounting

---

[46] The successor committee sidestepped the issue in paragraph 2.19 of its report: 'The board should maintain a sound system of internal control to safeguard shareholders' investment and the company's assets.' See Hampel (1998).

[47] CAD 02277.

[48] The jigsaw metaphor was also used in Macdonald and Beattie (1993).

and auditing requirements also being promulgated. Hosted by the FRC and chaired by Dearing, the group included Cadbury, Michael Chamberlain, chair of the CCAB, Allan Cook and Henry Gold, technical directors of the ASB and ICAEW respectively, Michael Lawrence, chair of the Hundred Group of Finance Directors,[49] Bill Morrison, APB chair, and David Tweedie, ASB chair. The group met initially on 30 June 1993 and again on 14 September 1993. At the September meeting[50] Lawrence reported the concern of members of the Hundred Group about the amount of material being issued. Dearing identified elements affecting what was perceived as 'overload', which related chiefly to the timing of issuing consultation documents, consultation periods, the timing of publication of final documents, and the time allowed before implementation was required. He thought that this could be eased by coordination between the bodies issuing papers for consultation. He referred in particular to the paper on internal control, exposure of which had been delayed following the previous meeting of the group. Lawrence responded that that paper went beyond the scope of Cadbury, dealing with internal control 'as a broad issue affecting the Boardroom as a whole', and it was misleading to regard it as a response to Cadbury: 'a body consisting solely of accountants had broadened the debate, without any authority to do so'.

---

[49] Later to become chief executive of the Stock Exchange.
[50] Unnumbered paper.

Chamberlain observed that, while there was concern about the widening of the scope of the paper, there was also a demand for guidance from those charged with implementing the Cadbury proposals. Lawrence reiterated that, although the Hundred Group supported Cadbury, the document on internal control 'would be seen as provocative since it would range over issues that were not purely financial, though prepared by accountants'. Gold pointed out that the paper was already the result of compromise with bodies such as the Institute of Internal Auditors, which thought it should have gone even further: the draft Report had referred to 'internal financial control', but the word 'financial' had been dropped in response to these bodies. The paper had, therefore, had to include a discussion of the scope of the directors' report on internal control, and the working group had concluded that it was sufficient for the directors to report on internal financial controls. Lawrence repeated that the correct response to the Cadbury recommendations would be to deal only with the financial aspects of internal control. On going concern guidance, there seemed to be less controversy, although Lawrence expressed some concern about the authority of any guidance to be issued. The meeting notes mention the difference of opinion between ICAEW and the APB noted above, but without comment.

The issue of overload was also pursued by the CBI. Howard Davies wrote to Cadbury[51] on 25 October 1993, sending a paper setting out in detail the CBI's concern

---

[51] CAD 02531.

about all the issues under review and emphasizing the problems that even large companies were experiencing in assimilating and responding to the raft of proposals. The CBI followed this up with a letter to Dearing observing that companies might have very few senior people able to respond to consultation documents and that developments to date suggested that the accountancy profession might have gone beyond the scope of the Cadbury Committee. The CBI also recommended that the bodies producing guidance should publish a joint programme of consultation for 1994.

The CBI views were discussed at the third meeting of the 'overload' group on 13 December 1993.[52] The issue of the internal control guidance had highlighted the underlying concern about the authority of the bodies providing guidance. Cadbury pointed out that the Committee had a 'fairly limited base of authority' and that 'it was important that the Committee's moral authority should not be undermined by a wrangle over one particular issue'. He believed that the problem was in part presentational and that the concern about the widening of the scope of the guidance might be alleviated by producing a shorter document in the form of a statement of principles. Gold 'sensed a resistance to the whole idea of reporting publicly on internal control'. He said that many leading companies already had systems in place to provide boards with assurance over internal control and that the concerns expressed might be prompted by

---

[52] CAD 02519.

fear of liability for directors and auditors resulting from public reporting. He suggested that any guidance produced should be presented as a document that would 'be useful for the internal use of companies, especially audit committees'.

A further lengthy discussion ensued in which Lawrence again reiterated concerns about the scope of the proposed guidance and that, although the issues covered by the paper were important, they should be discussed elsewhere and not be presented in the context of responding to the Cadbury recommendations, since they included non-financial internal control. The discussion concluded with agreement that the issue should be passed back to the Internal Control Working Group. As we have already seen, the discussion then came back to the Committee. The task undertaken by the Working Group on Internal Control should not be underestimated. A letter from Cole to the Committee members in July 1993 noted that at that point the document had been redrafted seventeen times.[53]

Beyond the Committee's Remit

Some issues arose during this period that reflected broader concerns about corporate governance than were

---

[53] CAD 02269. The issue of internal control was eventually dealt with by the publication by ICAEW in 1999 of 'Internal Control: Guidance for Directors', produced by a working party chaired by Sir Nigel Turnbull. See <http://www.icaew.com/en/library/subject-gateways/corporate-governance/codes-and-reports/turnbull-report> (accessed 7 December 2012).

covered by the Committee's terms of reference. On 22 December 1992 Arnold Ziff, chairman of Stylo plc, wrote to Cadbury pointing out that current Stock Exchange rules disadvantaged small shareholders, who had to wait longer for information, and that the Report's recommendation for companies to hold meetings with large shareholders would exacerbate this. Cadbury acknowledged this but justified the approach as beneficial for all:

I appreciate that there is a problem over the unequal treatment of individual and institutional shareholders…it is important to all concerned that the institutions should have regular contacts at the right level and take a more active interest in the companies in which they are investing our money than most of them have done in the past. The more seriously that the institutions take their responsibilities as shareholders in companies, the greater the benefit to the individual shareholders in those companies, since all shareholders have an equal interest in effective governance.[54]

He also noted that the rules on the announcement of results had not previously been flagged as an issue but he had asked for comment from the Stock Exchange. There is no record of this having been received.[55]

A paper by Charkham on the extension of the recommendations to large private companies was deferred until the November 1993 meeting. Although this was beyond

---

[54] CAD 02505.

[55] The development of the Stewardship Code reflects a continuing focus on board engagement with institutional investors rather than small shareholders, although the UK Shareholders Association campaigns on their behalf <http://www.uksa.org.uk/> (accessed 7 December 2012).

the Committee's terms of reference, Charkham argued that the accountability of a company should not depend only on quotation but that size and impact on society should be taken into account. He compared the UK system with that of unquoted companies in Germany, which were still required to have a supervisory board:

If we accept the idea in principle that the process of governance should reflect in some way the increased capacity of a company to inflict damage through inefficiency or avoidable demise, the instrument in the UK model which needs adapting is our unitary board. The UK tradition would seem to rule out a two tier system; and there is little current support for employee representation.

The logical approach would therefore be to extend the Cadbury Code to big companies—say those with more than 500 employees in the group. This would mean their having non-executive directors and audit committee...as the power of appointment would still rest with the shareholders, whose representatives would in many cases dominate the board, the whole exercise might appear to be pointless. Stooges, it is argued, would be chosen, to be used at random and dismissed at will. But it is not as simple as that. The background of the directors would be stated and could be ascertained by anyone *interested* in the company. Their dismissal or resignation could become matters of public interest...Such a system would be far from perfect but it would be better than what we have now.

De Trafford had responded with the view of the IoD,[56] pointing out that with unquoted companies there would

---

[56] CAD 02533.

be no body that would be able to exert the type of sanction that the Stock Exchange could exert over quoted companies: 'Acceptance of Jonathan's suggestion could therefore be taken as implying acceptance by the Committee of the need for legislative intervention.' It was agreed that the issue, and the extension of the Report to private companies, could be added to the agenda of the successor committee.[57]

Misunderstandings

In January 1994 a columnist for the *Independent on Sunday* commented on the draft guidance issued by the Working Group on Internal Control, stating incorrectly that this had been issued by the Cadbury Committee, that companies would be forced to comply with it, and that Cadbury himself had been engaging in private meetings with finance directors to advance the proposals. Cadbury's draft reply was measured but his anger was barely suppressed.[58]

On 17 February 1994 Cadbury gave two informal press briefings at the Stock Exchange, reporting on activity since the publication of the Report in December 1992. The minutes of the meeting on 23 February reported that these meetings 'had been

[57] CAD 01339 lists issues passed on to the successor committee.
[58] CAD 01365; there is no evidence that the draft was actually sent or that any reply or apology was received.

instigated on the advice of the Committee's PR consultants with a view to the press gaining a better appreciation of the Committee's current position and to try to defuse some of the more extreme comments being made'.[59] Cadbury was accompanied by Mike Sandland, Gina Cole, and Nicholas Walters, a PR consultant. The briefing prepared for Cadbury by Cole[60] emphasized the wide distribution of the final Report and its influence in South Africa, Canada, and Australia, as well as in the UK National Health Service, which was producing draft codes of conduct and accountability for NHS Boards. The briefing described the ongoing monitoring process in association with ABI and ICAEW. The press pack contained further details, including a selection of examples of corporate governance reporting by companies and copies of two newspaper articles relating to progress in the accountancy profession on developing guidance on the issues of internal control and going concern: an article by Gerry Acher, then head of audit and accounting at KPMG, which set out arguments against auditors reporting on internal control effectiveness, although supporting the spirit of the Cadbury recommendations in general,[61] and a second article by Michael Lawrence, chairman of the Hundred Group of Finance Directors, which similarly expressed support for the report's intentions but also concern

---

[59] CAD 02277.
[60] CAD 02273.
[61] 'Auditors and Internal Controls', *The Times*, 6 January 1994.

about the profession's progress in producing guidance, costs of implementation, and 'corporate overload'.[62] The inclusion of these particular articles seems significant, as they demonstrate some of the complexity of the issues and difficulty in achieving consensus among interested parties. This was perhaps an attempt to highlight the unhelpfulness of simplistic critical commentary based on unrealistic expectations of what the Code and recommendations could achieve.

Correction of misunderstandings and misinterpretation continued to be necessary. Later that year, Arthur Andersen published a summary of the interim results of a survey that they had funded, conducted by a professor at the University of Birmingham, of the views on the Code of the chief executives of Midlands-based quoted companies. The summary had a very negative spin: it stated that 'the survey reveals deep uncertainty and misgiving of both the use and value of non-executive directors...' and described the findings as 'a severe disappointment to those promoting the Cadbury Code as a means of achieving better corporate governance'. Not only did Cadbury challenge this interpretation: the author himself confirmed that he had not been involved in the production of the summary and added: 'In fact, I believe that the wording of the Executive Summary is completely misleading. It seems to set out to be deliberately provocative.

---

[62] 'Cadbury Risks Causing Indigestion in Boardrooms', *Financial Times*, 13 January 1994.

It is an interpretation of our results with which we do not agree.'[63]

Integrity of the Code

In April 1995 a challenge to the integrity of the Code came, somewhat surprisingly, from one of the sponsors. Ownership of the Code itself was effectively sited with the Stock Exchange, but monitoring compliance was not a task that the Stock Exchange had either the resources or the will to undertake, and this had never been the intention of the Committee. However, the Exchange was having to adapt in the face of competition from exchanges elsewhere, and rapidly changing technology and a change of chairman and chief executive seemed to signal an attempt for it to position itself as a stronger regulatory body. In 1994 John Kemp Welch took over from Hugh Smith as chairman, and Michael Lawrence, who had been chairman of the Hundred Group of Finance Directors while finance director at Prudential Corporation, became chief executive. In April 1995 Lawrence instituted a review of the Listing Rules, issuing a discussion document for comment, which, among a large number of proposed rule amendments, included proposals that were widely reported as undermining the Exchange's commitment to the Code by dropping the requirement for a statement of Code

---

[63] CAD 01329.

compliance[64] and incorporating a report by the directors on the effectiveness of the company's system of internal controls and a statement that the business is a going concern.

At the Committee meeting on 10 May 1995, Cadbury reported that the Exchange had confirmed that the requirement for a statement of Code compliance would be retained but the rationale for the incorporation into the Listing Rules of the sections of the Code relating to internal control and going concern remained unclear. The Head of Listing, Nigel Atkinson, had written to Cadbury indicating that these areas should be included as they had 'a clear investor protection role', but Cadbury observed that other parts of the Code, such as those relating to audit committees, would also fall into this category but were not to be included. Atkinson's letter also contained the comment: 'There is a view that the current approach to Cadbury should be changed.' The meeting minutes record Cadbury's terse observation that 'this begged the question of whose view this was, and to what end changes should be made'. Lipworth and Sarah Brown both reported differing impressions given by the chairman and chief executive of the Stock Exchange as to the intention of the changes. Hugh Smith's comments in the discussion suggested that, in his view, the Exchange was

[64] 'Cadbury Commitment Melts Away', *Investor Relations* (June 1995); Norma Cohen, 'Stock Exchange May Drop "Best Practice" Rule', *Financial Times*, 21 April 1995.

taking a very narrow view focused on investor protection when it should share the wider public interest of the Committee. The Committee agreed that it was important to establish the long-term objectives of the Exchange with regard to the Code, so that the successor committee would be clear on this.

A press release from the Stock Exchange on 24 May read:

The Exchange is delighted at the positive response by companies to the recommendations contained in the Cadbury Code. It shows the benefits of incorporating into the Exchange's listing rules those elements of other bodies' codes of best practice relating to investor protection. For the future we believe that targeting key areas for specific compliance in our rules may be a more sensible approach rather than the existing blanket rule re compliance, given that other bodies, such as the Greenbury Committee, are devising codes which may cover the same ground but potentially with a different approach. We are currently consulting with companies, member firms and other market practitioners on the subject.[65]

A meeting on 1 June 1995 was attended by Cadbury, Lawrence, Lipworth, and Kemp Welch. Lawrence explained that the Exchange's intentions had been misrepresented in the press,[66] that the compliance statement requirement would remain, and that the only element of the Code that would now be transferred to the Listing

---

[65] CAD 02319.

[66] In a handwritten note to Cole after this meeting, Cadbury wrote: 'The worrying point is that the Stock Exchange issues no corrections to the "misstatements" which appear in the Press' (CAD 02323).

Rules would be paragraph 4.6 relating to going concern. 'The logic of the move is that the going concern statement is crucial and should not be left open to compliance or non-compliance.' Concern remained among Committee members that including specific sections of the Code in the Listing Rules could weaken the integrity of the Code as a whole. Peace, now back at the DTI, wrote to Cadbury in August 1995 expressing the DTI view:

> we certainly want to see the Stock Exchange strengthen its position as a credible regulator...We are however more circumspect about the gradual incorporation of the main rules from the Code of Best Practice into the Listing Rules. If the Code is unpicked then it seems to me that the consensus that has built up around it would start to fall apart.[67]

In the event, the going concern statement requirement was incorporated into Amendment 5 to the Listing Rules issued in August 1995 but no other changes with regard to the Code were made at that time.[68]

As well as responding to issues raised, the Committee was also keeping a weather eye on the adoption of the Code and recommendations through a programme of active monitoring and research, which is examined in the next chapter.

---

[67] CAD 02325.

[68] Lawrence was sacked from his post as chief executive in January 1996: the reasons were never made clear, but press speculation suggested that in a push to reform he had 'antagonised a range of vested interests' (*Independent*, 5 January 1996).

6

Following Up: Early Adoption, Monitoring, and Research

In its Report, the original Committee had expressed its intention to support its successor body's activities by providing information about the early adoption of the Code:

The Committee will remain responsible for reviewing the implementation of its proposals until a successor body is appointed in two years' time, to examine progress and to continue the ongoing governance review. It will be for our sponsors to agree the remit of the new body and to establish the basis of its support. In the meantime a programme of research will be undertaken to assist the future monitoring of the Code. (Cadbury 1992: 11)

The programme of research comprised two strands: the work of the Monitoring Sub-Committee and a series of academic studies supported by ICAEW.

Dearing had met ICAEW representatives in May 1992 to discuss ways in which ICAEW could develop a research programme to follow up the Committee's work.[1] In January 1993, Cadbury wrote to Likierman,[2] explaining the proposals already discussed for the management of the ICAEW research programme but emphasizing that, although working closely with ICAEW, it was his view that the Committee should take responsibility for its own monitoring. He suggested that this could be achieved by establishing a computerized database of information drawn from published reports, which would show how companies were complying with the Code and recommendations. To manage this, he wanted to propose to the Committee the establishment of a Monitoring Sub-Committee, which would liaise with ICAEW and also establish a system for collecting monitoring data.

On 3 March 1993, at its first meeting after the publication of the final Report, the reconstituted committee discussed arrangements for monitoring adoption of the Code and recommendations and agreed to establish a Monitoring Sub-Committee (MSC) along the lines that Cadbury had envisaged, to be chaired by Likierman.[3] The proposed terms of reference agreed at that meeting were: to oversee the setting-up of a system for collecting monitoring data on the extent to which listed companies comply with the Code; and to liaise with the ICAEW Research Board and other bodies interested in financing research into compliance with the

---

[1] CAD 01307.
[2] Additional papers.
[3] CAD 02265.

Committee's recommendations.[4] Proposed members of the MSC were Likierman as chair, de Trafford, Hugh Smith, Macdonald, Charkham, Sandland, and Taylor, with Cole as secretary.

The first meeting of the MSC took place at the Stock Exchange on 31 March. Cole had drafted a paper[5] summarizing points for the MSC's consideration, which had been raised at the Committee meeting in March 1993, and also provided a note of organizations with the capability of monitoring Code compliance with whom the MSC might work. A lengthy discussion about the remit took place. Sandland thought that the remit was clear—to establish whether company behaviour had changed in response to the Code. Macdonald argued for a wider remit to explore some of the issues that had prompted the original setting-up of the Committee: 'for example, the need to penetrate the perceptions of both shareholders and analysts and gain a better understanding of their thinking; to find out, through the institutional shareholders, what systematic approaches are used by investors; to explore the market effect of compliance; and to study supervisory boards and see if there is a better model'.[6] It was eventually agreed that the remit should be wider rather than narrower and revisions to the proposed terms of reference would be referred back to the main Committee.

---

[4] Additional papers.
[5] Additional papers.
[6] Additional papers.

Further discussion ensued about the practicalities of monitoring, including the collection of the necessary data. It was initially decided that a questionnaire to be sent to institutional shareholders should be constructed. Over the next few weeks, however, the significant complexity of such a task became apparent, and plans were revised in the light of information received about ABI plans for a monitoring exercise on behalf of its members, for which they proposed to appoint a researcher. Discussions about cooperation with ABI continued during the summer, and at the September meeting it was agreed that the Committee should contribute funding to support this appointment. Detailed discussion of the proposed sample and the draft questionnaire continued; this eventually became a checklist, which the researcher completed by examining company reports and making direct enquiries, rather than an instrument to be sent to companies for completion.

Early results reported from other monitoring exercises were encouraging: for example, in September 1993 a survey by Coopers & Lybrand into the reaction of medium sized companies to the Code was published.[7] The report was based on questionnaires and interviews with a sample of thirty representatives from 'FT top 200 companies'. The respondents indicated that the Code was generally well accepted and that most companies, if not fully compliant, were already moving towards that position, but they also expressed considerable scepticism in answer to the question 'Will Cadbury work?' The report concluded: 'As one

[7] CAD 01327.

respondent put it: "Codes will not catch rogues!"' However, such surveys were based on limited data, and MSC members were concerned that their report should be based on a rigorous and robust methodology. This concern was reflected in the detailed attention paid to reports of the monitoring process at every meeting, but it was also agreed that information should be sought from other groups conducting monitoring exercises, particularly about the processes employed. The MSC meeting in February 1994 heard from representatives of NAPF about their monitoring activity, and David Tonkin, editor of *Company Reporting*, attended the meeting in May. The Cadbury Code had been the Issue of the Month in this publication in March.[8] Members of the MSC were critical of the approach taken in the analysis, which was viewed as mechanistic and seemed to suggest that non-compliance statements were negatively viewed, contradicting the spirit of the Code.

The non-compliance statement of Arlen plc in May 1994 attracted attention as the company declined to provide an explanation, commenting critically in its report on the cost of complying with the Code, resulting in the auditors (KPMG Peat Marwick) reporting that the compliance statement was inadequate. This was the first example of such an occurrence, and the issue was raised at the December 1994 meeting of the main Committee. Cole's note[9] said that Hugh Smith was strongly of the view that the institutional investors 'should be made to take action

---

[8] *Company Reporting*, 45 (March 1994).
[9] CAD 02311.

when a company in which they invest makes such a statement'. The MSC had suggested that the Committee should write a letter to the institutional investors to reinforce this, but this appears to have been considered unnecessary, since the meeting minutes record: 'It now appears that Arlen is likely to comply in future and there had been investor pressure for them to do so.'[10]

An interim report was presented to the main Committee at its December 1994 meeting.[11] At that point the ABI researcher had examined the reports of 631 companies reporting after 30 June 1993: all of these had made a statement of compliance or non-compliance and in only one case (Arlen) had the auditors considered the statement unsatisfactory.

The final compliance report covered a sample of 710 companies, including all the top 500. It was launched with a press briefing on 24 May 1995 by Cadbury accompanied by Charkham, Sandland, Taylor, and Richard Regan from the ABI. Cadbury explained that the research into compliance was undertaken to provide information for the successor committee in its consideration of the impact of the Code, but the Committee had then seen that the results would be of interest to a wider audience and could provide a benchmark for boards and shareholders against which to measure themselves, so the report had been sent to all listed company chairmen. The report indicated that information disclosure had increased in relation to the establishment of audit, nomination, and

[10] CAD 02285.
[11] CAD 02303.

remuneration committees, the number of independent non-executive directors, and the splitting of chairman/CEO roles (although this was not a Code requirement). Cadbury concluded with the observation: 'It will be up to the shareholders, both institutional investors and the smaller private investor, to put the information now available to them to constructive use.'[12]

Little attention has been paid to this study, and it is unclear whether the successor committee made use of it, as was the original intention, but, in describing in detail the methods used, it stands out from other monitoring reports published in the early days of adoption, such as the Coopers & Lybrand survey noted above and a report from PIRC also published in 1993.[13] The attention to detail revealed in the MSC minutes demonstrates a valiant effort to produce an objective assessment of the early adoption of the Code and recommendations, which is entirely consistent with the spirit in which the Committee operated.

ICAEW Research Programme

The academic research sponsored by ICAEW continued in parallel to the work of the MSC. The ICAEW research programme was managed by a sub-committee of its research board, with Likierman and Cole also attending meetings.

---

[12] Unnumbered paper, box 13.
[13] PIRC Corporate Governance Service, 'Meeting the Cadbury Challenge? A Summary of Trends towards Compliance with the Cadbury Committee Report on Corporate Governance' (July 1993).

Submissions of research proposals had been invited in the areas identified at the meeting in December 1992.[14] These were specified very broadly, and covered research into compliance with the Code, other than routine monitoring, as well as other aspects of corporate governance not addressed by the Committee. Examples of studies relevant to compliance proposed included: investigations of the characteristics of compliant and non-compliant companies; research into the economic consequences of compliance; and studies of the extent to which compliance was 'real' as opposed to 'cosmetic'.

At a meeting on 29 September 1993[15] nine of the fifteen submissions received from UK academics were referred for further consideration, with the remainder being rejected. Of the nine, six were eventually funded at a total cost of £43,356. The topics were: board structure and qualifications in firms gaining quotation in the UK; CEO remuneration and corporate governance; audit committees in small listed companies; corporate governance, internal controls, and the management audit; and two studies exploring the rise and role of institutional shareholders in corporate governance. All projects were completed by 1996 and formed the basis of a book published in 1997 (Keasey and Wright 1997).

Although the approval of the projects was noted by the Committee, no discussion of their outcomes was ever minuted, and it is not clear whether the findings of the projects

---

[14] CAD 01307.
[15] ICAEW Research Board records.

were fed into the deliberations of the successor committee.[16] These were, however, among the earliest studies of aspects of UK corporate governance to be published. The dearth of UK studies may explain why the Cadbury Committee seems to have made little reference to academic research in the course of its work, although Cadbury himself was aware of relevant US research as his annotations to various papers indicate, and he wrote an enthusiastic preface to an early comparative international study of boards (Demb and Neubauer 1992). The Committee's views about the value of non-executive directors and the role of audit committees were brought to the table initially based on their own experience, anecdotal reports, and implicit assumptions about best practice. These views were in the most part echoed in the submissions to the Committee, and, although their conclusions were contested by some commentators, there was surprisingly little criticism of the lack of underpinning objective evidence.[17]

It is clear that the work conducted by the Committee and the MSC in the post-report stage—the longer period of the Committee's life—was of great importance in embedding the ideas in the Code and recommendations,

---

[16] Tricker (1998: 2) commented on the Hampel Report: 'There is no evidence in the report that the Committee was aware of the now extensive body of research and academic knowledge on corporate governance around the world.'

[17] A study of audit committees in large UK companies was published by ICAEW in 1992 (Collier 1992), but no reference to this was found in the Cadbury archive, so there is no indication that the Committee drew on this information to support the audit committee recommendations. The 2003 Higgs Review of the role and effectiveness of non-executive directors was the first UK corporate governance report to commission specific research. See McNulty et al. (2005).

particularly the notion of 'comply or explain', which has since been widely adopted in other voluntary codes around the world. As we have seen, anxieties about how compliance would be enforced featured strongly in early reactions to the Code. Critics did not believe that companies had sufficient incentive to comply or that sanctions for non-compliance were severe enough. However, a point that often needed to be emphasized in the early days was that compliance was not mandatory: the statement of compliance was the key point, and companies were free to depart from the Code as long as they explained the reasons for non-compliance. The Committee envisaged this process as improving communication of information to investors, who could use the explanatory statement as the basis of a conversation with companies.

A similar approach was being adopted in Australia, where in 1990 a working group representing the Business Council of Australia, the Australian Stock Exchange (ASX), the Institute of Company Directors of Australia, and the Institute of Chartered Accountants of Australia had published a discussion paper entitled 'Corporate Practices and Conduct'.[18] This proposed a statement by directors in the annual report of support for the principles set out in the paper with a note of any departures from them and the reasons for such departures. This was later incorporated into the ASX Corporate Governance

---

[18] CAD 01029, copy of letter sent to Australian companies urging adoption.

Council's Principles and Recommendations and was described as 'if not, why not?' reporting.

The phrase 'comply or explain' does not appear anywhere in the Code or recommendations, although the concept clearly underpinned the Committee's thinking from the very beginning. A letter from Lickiss to Cadbury in September 1991[19] indicates that Cadbury had at an early stage asked the sponsors for their views on what outcomes the Committee might achieve: 'You asked me to record in a "rough and ready manner" my hopes and aspirations for the outcome...'. Lickiss emphasized that he was responding in a personal capacity and made various suggestions in relation to the role of independent non-executives and the separation of chair and CEO roles. He also proposed a statement of compliance: 'The directors should state categorically whether in their opinion and to the best of their knowledge and belief the accounts comply in all respects.'

The lasting impact of the idea of 'comply or explain' will be discussed in the final chapter.

The Successor

The Committee had made it clear that the Code of Best Practice should not be the last word on corporate governance and that there should be a process of regular review in the future.[20]

---

[19] CAD 01105.
[20] Reflecting on this in an article in 1998, Charkham (1998) thought that this was too soon.

Acceptance of the report's findings will mark an important advance in the process of establishing corporate standards. Our recommendations will, however, have to be reviewed as circumstances change and as the broader debate on governance develops. We will continue in existence as a Committee until a successor body is appointed, to act as a source of authority on our recommendations and to review their implementation. (Cadbury 1992: 9)

But, in spite of this clear intention, establishing a successor body was no easy task.

At the December 1994 meeting Lipworth reported on FRC discussions about the successor committee. It had been agreed that 'it should be a continuation of the existing committee with the addition of new members and under a new chairman. Its remit would be determined by its sponsors who were at present the FRC, LSE [London Stock Exchange], CBI, IoD and the accountancy profession.' He added that he was hoping to add representation from investors to the sponsors.[21]

The FRC hosted a meeting chaired by Lipworth on 29 January 1995 to 'take up the remit given to the FRC by paragraph 3.12 of the Cadbury Report to convene the Cadbury Committee sponsors in order to appoint a successor to the committee'.[22] The meeting was attended by John Kemp-Welch, Hugh Smith's successor as chairman of the London Stock Exchange; Roger Lawson, ICAEW president and chair of the CCAB; Michael Mander, chairman of the IoD, and Sir Bryan Nicholson, chairman of

---

[21] CAD 02285.
[22] CAD 02331.

the CBI. The following points were discussed: the need for a successor committee, sponsors, finance, membership, chairman, timing, and administration. In reviewing the need for a successor committee, it was noted: 'Although on one view the Cadbury Committee had largely completed its job, there were some aspects of unfinished business that needed to be pursued.' This 'unfinished business' was not specified, although it was noted that the recommendations on internal control and going concern had been implemented only recently and their effects remained to be seen. The main justification for the appointment of a successor committee appeared to be the observation that 'if no succession arrangements were set in hand any follow up action needed might fall to Government to pursue, which would be contrary to the aims and spirit of the Committee's report'. There is little sense of overwhelming enthusiasm to take up the baton from any of those attending the meeting.

It was agreed that the role of the sponsors should be to set the remit, appoint the members, and arrange financing, and that the sponsors would provide the core committee membership but membership would not be confined to them. But who should the sponsors be? Three points were made. Firstly, it was thought to be important that 'both sponsors and other members should be those with a real locus'.[23] Secondly, it was agreed that the

---

[23] This somewhat mysterious criterion was recorded as ruling out the RSA, which had sponsored the Tomorrow's Company inquiry into the role of business in a changing world, published in 1995.

government should not be a sponsor, since 'this would change the essentially private sector and self-regulatory nature of the committee'. Thirdly, it would not be appropriate to seek sponsorship from individual companies. It was agreed that the sponsors should be the interests represented at the meeting, together with ABI and NAPF if they were willing. It was also noted that, when a new chairman was appointed, the FRC would cease its sponsorship role.

The sponsors would be expected to provide finance, although the channel through which this could be achieved by the accountancy profession was not entirely clear. The ideal chairman was seen as the chairman of a major listed company, 'someone who still had his finger on the pulse'. Membership should not exceed eleven or twelve, to include representatives of the sponsors, a lawyer, some representation of smaller listed companies, and some individual listed company chairmen. Some continuity between the old and new committees would be ideal. Concerns about the authority of the committee appeared to surface in the discussion: it was thought important that representatives should be of sufficient status in terms of organizational roles and experience to counter any criticism from company chairmen that the committee did not understand the issues. It was also suggested that a more formal appointment procedure than for the original committee should be undertaken, possibly with the sponsors making formal appointments.

It was clear that defining the committee's remit would be a particular challenge. Should the remit be widened beyond the financial aspects of corporate governance? There was a sense that this constraint on the original committee had conveyed a misleading perception of the role of non-executive directors, with an emphasis on their monitoring role, which had led to the accusation that the recommendations would damage the principle of the unitary board. As well as following up the Cadbury Report recommendations, further issues had been suggested for the new committee's attention by various interests: these included directors' remuneration and the role of shareholders at annual general meetings. A period of 'reflection and absorption' was needed to assess the impact of the adoption of the Code, and this would affect the new committee's remit. It was suggested that the new committee should not start work until early in 1996, and there was some discussion about the existing Committee continuing a little further beyond the June 1995 deadline.

The final meeting of the Committee on the Financial Aspects of Corporate Governance took place on 10 May 1995 at the London Stock Exchange. All members were present, and a dinner followed. The matters discussed included the ongoing issue regarding the role of the Stock Exchange with regard to the Code, the compliance report produced by the Monitoring Sub-Committee, and the appointment of the successor committee. It was noted that the APB had produced a discussion paper on internal financial control effectiveness, an issue that would be pursued with the successor committee. The final minute reads: 'Sir Sydney

Lipworth proposed that a formal record should be made of the Committee's thanks to the Chairman for his masterful and outstanding chairmanship. Although sometimes touching on controversial issues, the Committee, under his chairmanship, had had a profound effect on both business confidence and business ethics.'[24]

Cadbury gave up the post of chair officially on 30 June 1995, although a press notice released by the FRC on 3 July noted that 'discussions have been held with a prospective chairman who is interested in principle in accepting the appointment but who is unable to commit himself until early September' and that 'Sir Adrian Cadbury has agreed to remain available, if need be, assisted by a small secretariat, until the new Committee has been established'. Robert Bruce in *The Times* noted that Cadbury's 'desire to see fair play' remained 'undimmed', as on 1 July he was to be found acting as a timekeeper at the Henley Royal Regatta.

A note made by Cole in March 1995[25] summarizes the cost of the Committee's operations. Over the four years from June 1991 to May 1995 the total income from the sponsors was £280,000, of which approximately £250,000 had been spent to that date. The Committee secretary's salary accounted for almost half of this (a full-time post from May 1991 to December 1992, part-time thereafter). The rest of the expenditure comprised

---

[24] CAD 02289.
[25] CAD 02335.

18 per cent on public relations, 14 per cent on commissioned research, and the remainder on other costs such as stationery, printing, books and publications, travelling expenses and entertainment, none of which exceeded 5 per cent of the total.

The Committee's commitment to provide evidence of Code adoption for its successor laid the foundations for the ongoing review that had always been envisaged. The Code and recommendations were seen as the start of an ongoing evolutionary process, which has continued over the subsequent years. In the next chapter we consider this legacy and its influence.

7

What Happened Next

In his Gresham College lecture, Cadbury (1998) reflected: 'We delivered our Report and Code of Best Practice...and imagined that this would be the end of the matter and that we could retire to cultivate our gardens. This, however, was not to be because by then corporate governance...had become a matter of considerable public interest worldwide.' As we have seen, the longer part of the Committee's existence followed the launch of the Report and Code. During this period, members focused on clarification in response to queries about the Code relating to interpretation and implementation, the monitoring of the adoption of the Code, the identification of problem areas for the successor body to consider, and generally keeping the flame alive. As chairman, Cadbury rapidly became the public face of corporate governance around the world, travelling widely to address conferences and spending time giving interviews to journalists from publications ranging from local newspapers to widely read practitioner journals. By 1998, Cadbury noted: 'I have to date visited 28 countries in the governance cause, some of them more than once.'[1]

The Ongoing Agenda

Companies exist in an economic environment that may change rapidly, to which they need to adapt. Board arrangements suitable at one point in time may be inappropriate at another. Corporate governance requirements need to recognize and accommodate such change. The Committee's view was always that one size does not fit all and that best practice is an evolving notion. Its insistence that the impact of the Code should be reviewed by a successor committee is clear evidence of this. The Committee had always envisaged that the Code would develop, initially through the work of the successor committee and that of other groups working on areas of concern beyond the remit of the Committee. As well as the ongoing work on internal control reporting and on going concern within the accountancy profession, the IoD and the CBI both continued to address corporate governance issues of particular importance to their members.

The minutes of the February 1994 meeting note that Cadbury drew attention to an IoD paper on 'Good Practice for Boards of Directors' on which de Trafford

---

[1] Cadbury (2000). In this article Cadbury also wrote that he was retiring from the field: at the time of writing (December 2012) he is still speaking and writing on the topic.

commented that 'the IoD was in no way trying to "outdo" Cadbury, but that where Cadbury could be equated with integrity, the IoD could be equated with enterprise'.[2] In January 1995 the CBI set up a Study Group on directors' remuneration, chaired by Sir Richard Greenbury,[3] in response to public concern about high levels of executive pay, prompted in particular by the reported 75 per cent increase in pay of Cedric Brown, chief executive of the newly privatized British Gas Corporation. Although the group was working at the same time as the Committee, there seems to have been little recognition of any shared concern: the only mention in the archive is in a note provided for Cadbury,[4] presumably by Cole, before the May 1995 press briefing. The note clearly distances the work of the two groups, emphasizing that the Cadbury Committee had not given evidence to Greenbury and that Cadbury himself had no knowledge of what the Study Group would recommend or how such recommendations would be taken forward.

The Study Group's remit was: 'To identify good practice in determining Directors' remuneration and prepare a Code of such practice for use by UK PLCs' (Greenbury 1995: 9). The report was published in July 1995. It lists the members[5] but does not indicate how they were

---

[2] This observation seems to presage the approach of the successor committee.
[3] Then chairman and chief executive of Marks and Spencer.
[4] CAD 02321.
[5] Taylor was the only member of the Cadbury Committee to have been a member of the Study Group. Hogg was also a member.

chosen, although NAPF and ABI each nominated a member. No indication is provided as to how the Group set about its work beyond the statement that 'the Group was grateful to receive advice from a wide variety of organisations, including companies, shareholder bodies, the TUC and from individuals. These have greatly assisted our deliberations' (Greenbury 1995: 9). Appendix III of the report lists contributors to the Group, predominantly the chairmen and senior board members of UK plcs. The report recommended the establishment of remuneration committees comprised of independent non-executive directors, together with extended disclosure of directors' remuneration details. Subsequently the Combined Code drew on these recommendations.[6] While neither Cadbury himself nor the Committee seems to have provided input to these deliberations, Cadbury included in his submission to the successor committee a comment on what he viewed as a significant error in the Greenbury Report: 'A1 states that the remuneration committee should determine on behalf of the board the policy on directors' pay and the individual pay packages of directors. This is constitutionally wrong. The decision should be that of the board, however much it may be guided by its committee.'[7] The Greenbury Study Group reported during the hiatus between the end of the Cadbury Committee's work and the appointment of the successor committee.

[6] Links to subsequent corporate governance reports and versions of the Combined Code can be found at <http://www.jbs.cam.ac.uk/cadbury/report/furtherreports.html> (accessed 5 December 2012).

[7] Unnumbered paper, box 13.

As we have seen in Chapter 6, the establishment of the latter took some time.

The Successor Body: The Committee on Corporate Governance (the Hampel Committee)

The minutes of the final meeting of the Committee on 10 May 1995[8] included an update from Lipworth on the convening of the successor body. The sponsors of the Committee had met the chairman of ABI and NAPF to agree on a draft of the remit of the successor committee. Lipworth was acting as convenor, but the FRC would not be a sponsor. 'It was likely that the word "financial" would be dropped from the new Committee's title. The view was held that it should not be concerned with governance in the abstract but governance with the aim of investor protection.' The new committee would have twelve members plus a chairman. Each of the financial sponsors would nominate one person, 'although the person would not necessarily be a representative of that organisation'. The chairmanship had yet to be determined and 'was being considered by one potential candidate'. On 3 July 1995 the sponsors of the new committee were announced as the FRC,[9] the London Stock Exchange, the CBI, the IoD, CCAB, NAPF, and ABI.

---

[8] CAD 02289.

[9] CAD 02331. Notes of a meeting on 29 January 1995 record that the FRC's sponsorship would end when the successor committee was finally in place.

Finally, on 22 November 1995, the FRC sent out a press notice announcing that the Cadbury Committee would be succeeded by the Committee on Corporate Governance, to be chaired by Sir Ronald Hampel, chairman of ICI, with the following members: Michael Coppel (chairman, Airspring plc), Michael Hartnall (finance director, Rexam plc), Christopher Haskins (chairman, Northern Foods plc), Giles Henderson (senior partner, Slaughter and May), Sir Nigel Mobbs (chair and chief executive, Slough Estates plc),[10] Tony Richards (director, Henderson Crosthwaite Ltd), Tom Ross (director, Alexander Clay and Partners), Sir David Simon (chair, BP plc), Peter Smith (Coopers & Lybrand), David Thomas (director, Equitable Life), and Clive Thompson (chief executive, Rentokil plc). No information was provided on the process of appointment of members, nor was this explained in the final report.

In October 1996 the Hampel Committee sought views on the Code and recommendations. It consulted widely and, following the practice of its predecessor, issued both a preliminary report for comment and a final report.

Before the preliminary report the Committee issued a questionnaire in answer to which over 140 submissions were received, and members of the Committee took part in over 200 individual and group discussions. We received a further 167 written

---

[10] An interesting choice, since the Cadbury Report recommended splitting the roles. Mobbs relinquished the chief executive role in 1996 but remained executive chairman until his retirement in 2005.

submissions on the preliminary report and we have had a substantial number of further discussions. In total 252 organisations or individuals responded in writing to one or both of these consultations. (Hampel 1998: 5)

Cadbury provided several pages of detailed comment,[11] addressing in particular the ongoing issues of reporting on internal control, differentiation on the basis of size, board structure, and the split between the chairman and CEO roles. There is a strong emphasis in his response that the Committee had not wanted to add to the burden of boards and had been keen to remain within the existing legal framework.

The Hampel Report was published in January 1998. It was explicitly in favour of correcting what was viewed as an imbalance between accountability and enterprise, as shown in its opening paragraph:

The importance of corporate governance lies in its contribution both to business prosperity and to accountability. In the UK the latter has preoccupied much public debate over the past few years. We would wish to see the balance corrected. Public companies are now among the most accountable organisations in society. They publish trading results and audited accounts; and they are required to disclose much information about their operations, relationships, remuneration and governance arrangements. We strongly endorse this accountability and we recognise the contribution to it made by the Cadbury and Greenbury committees. But the emphasis on accountability

---

[11] Unnumbered paper, box 13.

has tended to obscure a board's first responsibility—to enhance the prosperity of the business over time. (Hampel 1998: 7)

The original expression of the committee's views on this was even stronger. In the committee's preliminary report, published in August 1997, the second sentence of this extract read: 'In the UK the latter has preoccupied much public debate over the past few years to the detriment of the former' (Hampel 1997: 1.1). The final report of the Hampel Committee was followed in June 1998 by the first version of the Combined Code, described as 'Principles of Good Governance and Code of Best Practice. Derived by the Committee on Corporate Governance from the Committee's Final Report and from the Cadbury and Greenbury Reports.'[12]

The Hampel Report identified 'box-ticking' as a problem:

1.12 Companies' experience of the Cadbury and Greenbury codes has been rather different. Too often they believe that the codes have been treated as a set of prescriptive rules. The shareholders or their advisers would be interested only in whether the letter of the rule had been complied with—yes or no. A 'yes' would receive a tick—hence the expression 'box-ticking' for this approach. (Hampel 1998: 10)[13]

---

[12] <http://www.ecgi.org/codes/documents/combined_code.pdf> (accessed 5 December 2012).

[13] Note that this concern is with the interpretation by shareholders of company compliance with the Code, not with a 'box-ticking' approach to compliance by the companies themselves.

The evidence on which the committee based this conclusion is unclear, although the view that explanations of non-compliance would be ignored had been expressed earlier—for example, in the publication 'Company Reporting', which had aroused the concern of the Monitoring Sub-Committee noted in the previous chapter. The Coopers & Lybrand survey of September 1993 also indicated that some companies believed that a stigma attached to making a statement of non-compliance. In an attempt to address the 'box-ticking' problem, the Combined Code distinguished between principles and the guidelines of the Cadbury Code: 'With guidelines, one asks "How far are they complied with?"; with principles, the right question is "How are they applied in practice?"' (Hampel 1998: 16). In considering the unresolved issue of internal control reporting, the Hampel Committee appeared to dilute the Cadbury recommendations. Summarizing the state of play and its own thinking,[14] the Hampel Committee downplayed the Cadbury recommendation that directors should report on the effectiveness of internal controls and the Combined Code dealt with the problem thus:[15]

D.2 Internal Control
Principle The board should maintain a sound system of internal control to safeguard shareholders' investment and the company's assets.

---

[14] Hampel (1998: 52–4).
[15] <http://www.ecgi.org/codes/documents/combined_code.pdf> (accessed 5 December 2012).

Code Provisions

D.2.1 The directors should, at least annually, conduct a review of the effectiveness of the group's system of internal control and should report to shareholders that they have done so. The review should cover all controls, including financial, operational and compliance controls and risk management.[16]

The issue of internal control reporting was finally addressed by an ICAEW internal control working party chaired by Nigel Turnbull (then chairman of Rank Group plc), which in 1999 published guidance for directors.[17] This guidance has been regularly reviewed by the FRC in the light of practical experience,[18] as has the Combined Code—now the UK Corporate Governance Code.[19]

The failure of the US energy corporation Enron, in 2001, prompted the DTI to commission Derek Higgs[20] to review the role of non-executive directors. Higgs reported on this in January 2003. Some aspects of his recommendations have been incorporated in guidance for

---

[16] This is the first explicit mention of risk management in the context of internal control. See Spira and Page (2003) and Page and Spira (2004) for further discussion.

[17] 'Internal Control: Guidance for Directors on the Combined Code' <http://www.ecgi.org/codes/documents/turnbul.pdf> (accessed 5 December 2012).

[18] See Spira and Gowthorpe (2008) for discussion of the review consultation process.

[19] For the most recent version of the Code, see <http://www.frc.org.uk/corporate/ukcgcode.cfm> (accessed 5 December 2012).

[20] Higgs was a chartered accountant who had worked in banking for many years and at the time of his appointment had recently stepped down from the chairmanship of Prudential. He was knighted in 2004 and went on to chair Alliance and Leicester until his death in 2008.

non-executive directors issued by the FRC. The report[21] was notable for its direct commissioning of academic research to inform its conclusions.[22] Similarly, a group under the chairmanship of Sir Robert Smith was set up by the FRC in 2002 at the request of the Co-ordinating Group on Audit and Accounting Issues (CGAA), the body established by the government to oversee and coordinate the response in the UK to the issues raised by recent major corporate failures in the USA. The Smith group produced guidance on audit committees, designed to assist boards in implementing the Combined Code provisions in this area, and this is also regularly reviewed alongside the Code itself.

Academic Perspectives

The involvement of academics in UK corporate governance policy-making has been limited. Likierman's membership of the Cadbury Committee remains unusual, as does the active engagement with the ICAEW research programme. Subsequent groups and committees have rarely included the formal appointment of academics, and, apart from Higgs, there appears to have been no direct commissioning of academic work. Some academics respond to FRC consultations, but it is unclear what influence their responses have, if any. However,

---

[21] Higgs (2003).
[22] See McNulty et al. (2005).

corporate governance issues are of considerable interest to academics in a variety of disciplines, and a significant body of academic literature has developed, supported by conferences and journals dedicated to the subject.

The earliest academic comment on the Committee's work came from legal scholars. As might be expected, they expressed a preference for legal solutions to the issues addressed. Freedman (1993) asserted that the lack of a fundamental review of business law had left a vacuum that the accountancy profession was attempting to fill. Her main concern was that the Committee's work had excused the government from considering issues such as the role of non-executive directors and the potential value of the two-tier board within the legislative framework and that future debate may have been stifled. The threat of future legislation if the Code was not supported implied an undesirable view of the role of law:

we see law depicted as a negative influence summoned up to do the unpleasant duty of enforcing detailed requirements: a device which might actually become an obstacle to enterprise, so that it is better avoided. The notion that law might have a positive and profound role in formulating guidelines for corporate society is not even contemplated. (Freedman 1993: 294–5)

Dine (1994) described a research project[23] designed to investigate the Committee's claim that proposals had

[23] The paper reports the first phase of a project that does not appear to have been continued.

received majority support, to 'evaluate the methodology used by the Committee and to gather material on the debate about corporate governance'. The researchers wrote to those named as respondents to the draft Report asking for copies of their submissions, receiving 'approximately' 130 of the 'over 200' responses received by the Committee. It is not clear how the material was analysed: selected responses are discussed. The appendix to the article compared the draft and final reports but does not appear, as claimed, to provide a 'detailed grid of the "meat" of the responses'. The researchers identified overwhelming support for the exercise but noted that 'support for the detailed recommendations was much thinner on the ground'. Dine questioned whether a committee 'sitting in private and issuing a report purportedly supported by a "consensus" of views was the best way to arrive at an improved system of governance'. Like Freedman, Dine expressed concern that future debate on corporate governance issues would be stifled.

Belcher (1995) asserted that

regulation by the market in the case of the Cadbury Code of Best Practice will be ineffective because creative compliance will ensure that disclosures in the compliance statement contain little useful information. It is suggested that the incentives created by the obligation to make a compliance statement are for management to creatively comply with this obligation by creatively complying with the Cadbury Code itself. If this form of creative compliance occurs, the market may not be able to make a 'correct' response. The response may be to the corporate governance which appears to be in place rather than to that which is actually in place. The disclosures which are made by the directors are more likely to open expectations gaps than to allow informed shareholders to put appropriate pressure on directors. (Belcher 1995: 342)

Subsequent assessments suggest that these predictions may have been excessively negative.

More substantial empirical studies of the impact of adoption followed as data became available. Conyon and Mallin (1997) provided an early summary of evidence of compliance, drawing on the Monitoring Sub-Committee report and reports produced by Touche Ross in 1993 and 1994, KPMG in 1995, and PIRC in 1995, as well as a survey by Conyon in 1995. They focused on the adoption of the recommended board committees, noting that progress in establishing audit and remuneration committees had been substantial. Nomination committees, however, which were not required by the Code, had not developed to the same degree, and the authors considered this to be a significant governance weakness. They also noted that the proportion of non-executives among board members was increasing.

Weir and Lang (2000) studied links between compliance and performance but observed that 'the results show that complete compliance with the model proposed by Cadbury does not appear to result in superior performance when compared to the performance achieved by either partial or non compliance'.

Peasnell, Pope, and Young (2000) made the earliest attempt to provide an empirical investigation of changes in the level of monitoring by non-executive directors following the introduction of the Code. They examined the relationship between board composition (defined as the ratio of non-executive directors to board size) and earnings management (defined as abnormal working capital accruals). They noted that earnings management activity appeared in both periods but concluded that their results suggested that non-executive directors were playing a greater role in constraining earnings management in the post-Cadbury period. They were, however, careful to point out that no direct causal link could be identified and there could be other factors, beside Code adoption, influencing this change.

Dedman (2002: 350) provided a comprehensive overview of research into the impact of the Code and recommendations, noting that

existing research fails to find any direct relationship between the number of non-executives on UK boards and the value of the firm. This is consistent with the proposition that most boards were already well structured prior to Cadbury and implies that simple averaging of share price responses to such announcements is unlikely to reveal any effect. It may also be the case that those firms who would enjoy a share price increase on compliance with this aspect of the Code are still failing to comply... there is some evidence that restructuring the board to comply with Cadbury improves board oversight in several respects. There is evidence that accounting manipulation is reduced and that top executives are more likely to be disciplined for poor performance.

Jones and Pollitt (2002, 2004) compared the developments up to the time of the Higgs Review, identifying the influences on the various reporting groups. They observed that 'the Cadbury Report stands out among its successors as having a high quality process of investigation in the face of varied and strong influencer interest and in coming to and implementing radical yet realistic proposals' (Jones and Pollitt 2004: 163). A particular focus of academic research has been the effect of the principle of 'comply or explain', which is discussed in more detail in the final chapter.

All of the issues identified at the time of the Cadbury Report—directors' pay and the role of responsibilities of institutional investors, as well as reporting on internal control and going concern—remain a focus of continuing concern and the guidance provided is subject to regular review by the FRC, as is the Code itself. None of the subsequent groups charged with considering these ongoing issues has provided conclusive answers: this reflects the need, which the Cadbury Committee had emphasized, for continued review of the issues in the light of the practical experience of company boards and investors and the current business environment. The arena for debate opened up by the Committee's work has enabled discussions to continue, moving forward on the basis of the conclusions of each group and review, even though resolution of these problems remains elusive.

Owen (2011: 75), in an overview of changes in Britain's boards of directors from 1960 to 2010, concluded: 'There is no case for radical changes in the British corporate governance system...The challenge now is to make the existing system work better.' The Committee established an approach of incremental progress rather than drastic change: in the next chapter we reflect further on its legacy.

8

The Cadbury Contribution: Conversations, Codes, Consensus

Even before the formal conclusion of the Committee's work, the extent of the influence of its proposals was already becoming visible. In the press briefing of February 1994, an update on the second stage of the Committee's work included a note that the Report and Code had influenced the work of the King Committee in South Africa, the Toronto Stock Exchange Committee on Corporate Governance and developments in Australia; they had also generated interest in the UK public sector with the development of draft Codes of Conduct and Accountability for NHS Boards.[1] Soon after that, Belcher (1996) noted the diffusion of Code principles to the NHS and housing associations. By 2000, Cadbury could see the adoption of governance codes across the world,

---

[1] CAD 02273.

modelled on the Committee's work, with many drawing on his personal advice.[2]

Some members of the Committee—Charkham, Macdonald, and Cadbury himself—continued to write about its impact, and we have drawn on their publications in assessing the impact of the Committee's work, as well as the archive papers, press, and academic commentary. Others have shared with us their memories and reflections, which provide a further insight into their experience of the Committee's work. Overall, we see the Committee's contribution to comprise three closely linked themes: conversations, codes, and consensus.

Conversations

The catalyst for the Committee's establishment was, as we have seen in Chapter 2, discussion over dinner. Our interviewees' memories of these early conversations indicate that they set the tone for the Committee's deliberations and were thus of great importance. This particularly British method of dealing with issues of concern by gathering the great and the good at the dinner table also reflects, in this case, a significant institutional weakness: at the time there was no structure within which concerns

---

[2] See, e.g., the acknowledgement of his advice in The King Code of Governance for South Africa 2009, p. 4 <http://african.ipapercms.dk/IOD/KINGIII/kingiiicode/> (accessed 7 December 2012). See also Cheffins (2000).

about corporate governance could be comprehensively addressed. The legislative framework of the Companies Act focused on the individual director's duties rather than on the board of directors as a whole. Although the Committee's sponsors were respected organizations, it had no 'umbrella', as Charkham later observed:

The UK [corporate governance] system has generally not depended on primary or even secondary legislation, but on a mixture of both with rules made by various non-statutory bodies, some of which may, like the Stock Exchange, work under the umbrella of some legislation...some, like the Cadbury Committee, with no umbrella at all. (Charkham and Simpson 1999: 42)

Discussion over dinner may not appear to be the most efficient way of conducting business, but in this instance it proved to be a useful mechanism through which the issues requiring action were drawn to the attention of those in a position to address them. If those dinners had not taken place, it is difficult to see how the different groups concerned about corporate governance issues at the time might have found a way to integrate their ideas: the establishment of the Committee provided a useful focus for the varying conversations taking place and a means of achieving some sort of consensus among differing perspectives. However, although the Committee sponsors were respected organizations, this lack of an institutional 'umbrella' was reflected in the difficulties the Committee faced in defining its remit and the continuing need, keenly appreciated by its chair, to ensure that the Committee's processes conferred credibility and legitimacy on its conclusions.

Conversation also played a significant role in the Committee's deliberations. As the archive reveals, Cadbury and Peace took great pains to ensure that a wide range of views was captured through correspondence and informal meetings, as well as through the formal consultation process. It seems that such an approach had much to offer in terms of consensus building, because it allowed for the development of ideas through dialogue about matters raised with interested individuals and groups, some of whom might not feel directly represented by the Committee membership.

A Committee member reflected on the working process that was established:

it was essentially a body that everybody was contributing to. It worked informally...very friendly...room for everybody to have their fair shout. Adrian allowed virtually unstructured discussion round an agenda paper consisting of the points that we were going to look at. And after two meetings with this I thought we are never going to get anywhere at all with this. And at the end of the second meeting he said 'Would you like me to go away and produce a draft of the first section?'[3]

Macdonald (1997), in reflecting on the Committee's work, noted that the Committee was seeking greater clarity about roles and responsibilities at board level. He observed that such discussions had not taken place

---

[3] Interviewee S.

in the past, possibly because of the difficulty of raising issues without being seen to criticize the competence or integrity of board members. The Committee thus opened up this dialogue *within* companies by requiring boards to address the Code requirements and recommendations.[4]

The Committee's Report and recommendations also opened up a broader discussion, encompassing other interest groups such as policy-makers, regulators, and professional bodies. Much of this conversation has centred on the principle of 'comply or explain'.

The 'Comply or Explain' Conversation

The principle of comply or explain, central to the Code of Best Practice, was designed to promote dialogue between boards and shareholders. The principle has been widely copied in other voluntary codes around the world.[5] As we have seen, anxieties about how compliance would be enforced featured strongly in early reactions to the Code. Critics did not believe that companies had sufficient

---

[4] This aspect of the influence of the Code has recently been explored by Roberts (2012: 198), who observed: 'reported compliance (or explanation) tells us little of how the Code shapes or conditions actual board behaviour and culture'. His study identified two modes of compliance: 'defensive', with an emphasis on maintaining external legitimacy through compliance, and 'extensive', where compliance was complementary to a more strategic board focus. See also the longitudinal study of board behaviour conducted by Pye et al. (2012).

[5] See, e.g., Aguilera and Cuervo-Cazurra (2009).

incentive to comply or that sanctions for non-compliance were severe enough.[6]

A point that often needed to be emphasized in the early days was that compliance itself was not mandatory: the statement of compliance was the key requirement and companies were free to depart from the Code as long as they explained the reasons for non-compliance. The Committee envisaged this process as improving the communication of information between boards and investors, who could use the information disclosed to engage in conversation with companies. However, we have seen that this approach had, from the very start, raised concerns that a statement of non-compliance would trigger negative market reaction rather than dialogue.

A Committee member reflected on this:

we were clear that we wanted this to be something which was the basis for good practice and not in any sense a restrictive framework. And that was really important. Maybe we got that wrong, and maybe we didn't quite understand that people would prefer to have something where they could tick a box rather than have the discretion...giving them a responsibility for something which we thought was a kind of privilege— in a sense they regarded it as yet another obligation to make another damned difficult decision. So I think that's the bit that I remember very clearly we were surprised at.[7]

---

[6] In the early period of adoption, companies benefited from the reputational advantage conferred by compliance: see <http://www.lens-library.com/mckinsey.html> (accessed 7 December 2012).

[7] Interviewee L.

Academic research has explored the impact of 'comply or explain' and has suggested changes to improve its effectiveness.

Arcot, Bruno, and Faure-Grimaud (2010) analysed UK data from 1998 to 2004 to determine the impact of the 'comply or explain' regime. While noting an increasing trend for companies to comply with the Code, they found that the quality of explanations of non-compliance was poor. They demonstrated that more attention was paid by the market to compliance or non-compliance than to explanations and that intervention by shareholders generally followed poor performance and related to compliance rather than a pre-emptive stance taken on the basis of explanations. They concluded:

The Combined Code asks companies to either apply its provisions, or to explain why they do not. To be precise, both are valid ways of complying. It would therefore be more accurate, we feel, to refer to the approach as 'Apply or Explain', as this is what companies are asked to do. This admittedly minor change of terminology may help to promote the view amongst shareholders that greater attention has to be paid to explanations. It would recognize explicitly that companies that do one or the other de facto comply. (Arcot et al. 2010: 200)

This proposition has been explored to some extent in other countries where a similar code approach has been adopted. Variations in the wording exist, although the underlying principle of disclosure remains the same. King III sets this out clearly:

Internationally, the 'comply or explain' principle has also evolved into different approaches. At the United Nations, for instance, it was ultimately agreed that the UN code should be on an 'adopt or explain' basis. In the Netherland Code the 'apply or explain' approach was adopted. We believe that this language more appropriately conveys the intent of the King Code from inception rather than 'comply or explain'. The 'comply or explain' approach could denote a mindless response to the King Code and its recommendations whereas the 'apply or explain' regime shows an appreciation for the fact that it is often not a case of whether to comply or not, but rather to consider how the principles and recommendations can be applied. King III, therefore, is on an 'apply or explain' basis and its practical execution should be addressed as follows:

It is the legal duty of directors to act in the best interests of the company. In following the 'apply or explain' approach, the board of directors, in its collective decision-making, could conclude that to follow a recommendation would not, in the particular circumstances, be in the best interests of the company. The board could decide to apply the recommendation differently or apply another practice and still achieve the objective of the overarching corporate governance principles of fairness, accountability, responsibility, and transparency. Explaining how the principles and recommendations were applied, or, if not applied, the reasons, results in compliance. In reality, the ultimate compliance officer is not the company's compliance officer or a bureaucrat ensuring compliance with statutory provisions, but the stakeholders.[8]

Moore (2009) argued that the practical effect of comply or explain was compromised by three factors: the

---

[8] See The King Code of Governance for South Africa 2009 <http://www.ecgi.org/codes/documents/king3.pdf> (accessed 7 December 2012).

increasingly prescriptive provisions of iterations of the Code; the continuing 'box-ticking' approach adopted by 'key financial market actors', including institutional investors, corporate governance advisory firms, and credit rating agencies; and the boilerplate approach by boards to preparing statements of non-compliance. Moore's suggestions for shifting the attention of the market to evaluating non-compliance explanations focused on a rewording of the Code and some incorporation of its requirements into statute. An EU report in 2009 on Monitoring and Enforcement Practices in Corporate Governance in the Member States indicated broad support for comply or explain from investors, companies, and regulators but proposed that it could be strengthened:

The comply-or-explain approach formally adopted by the European Commission in 2006 enjoys wide acceptance by the corporate as well the institutional investor community. However, its practical implementation suffers some deficiencies, mainly in the form of an unsatisfactory level and quality of information on deviations by companies and a low level of shareholder monitoring. These issues could be remedied by strengthening the role of market-wide monitors and statutory auditors, creating a reporting framework to ensure comprehensive and qualitative disclosure by companies, and by developing a comply-or-explain regime for institutional investors. The comply-or-explain regime should not be abandoned. It should be strengthened.[9]

---

[9] Study on Monitoring and Enforcement Practices in Corporate Governance in the Member States, p. 18 <http://ec.europa.eu/internal_market/company/docs/ecgforum/studies/comply-or-explain-090923_en.pdf> (accessed 7 December 2012).

Seidl, Sanderson, and Roberts (2012), in a study of UK and German compliance statements, developed an extended taxonomy of explanations, linking these to the tactics employed by companies to establish legitimacy; they also considered the nature of regulatory responses.

The 'comply or explain' conversation necessarily encompasses regulators, but their involvement does not always imply a move away from self-regulation. Prompted by the EU discussions, the FRC organized a series of meetings between companies and investors to discuss what constitutes an explanation, concluding that:

there was agreement that explanations should be full and include reference to context and coherent rationale. They should explain how the company is fulfilling the relevant principle of the Code and also whether deviation from its provisions is time limited. Ideally explanations should be sufficiently full to meet the needs of those shareholders who could not simply call up the company and ask for information, but larger shareholders also saw them as the foundation for further dialogue that should engender trust.

…Shareholders were clear that a company was still in compliance with the code if it chose to deviate from one or more of its provisions and made a full and ample explanation. All participants agreed that companies had to deliver on the main principles, which were not negotiable. However, the principles were expressed in general terms which allowed some latitude in their implementation. This was a great resilient strength and one that participants agreed we should cling to. Used properly, the Code-based 'comply or explain' approach can deliver greater transparency and confidence than formal regulation which is purely a matter of compliance.[10]

This debate was developed further by the publication by ABI in December 2012 of a report proposing six criteria for the assistance of companies in preparing explanations that would meet investor expectations.[11]

Promoting engagement through dialogue rather than 'box-ticking' by investors is a continuing aspiration, as shown by the recommendations of the UK Stewardship Code[12] and the Walker Review.[13] The impact of the concept of 'comply or explain' was effectively summarized by the contributors to a set of essays published by the FRC in November 2012 to celebrate the twentieth anniversary of the publication of the Cadbury Code.[14] While these praise the intention behind the concept and identify the benefits that the implementation of the Code has brought, some critical observations in these essays signal

[10] FRC, 'What Constitutes an Explanation under "Comply or Explain"?' <http://www.frc.org.uk/getattachment/590dd61a-d3b1-4a2e-a214-90f17453fa24/What-constitutes-an-explanation-under-comply-or-explain.aspx> (accessed 7 December 2012).

[11] ABI, 'Comply or Explain: Investor Expectations and Current Practice' <http://www.abi.org.uk> (accessed 14 December 2012).

[12] The UK Stewardship Code <http://www.frc.org.uk/Our-Work/Codes-Standards/Corporate-governance/UK-Stewardship-Code.aspx> (accessed 7 December 2012).

[13] The Walker Review <http://webarchive.nationalarchives.gov.uk/+/http:/www.hm-treasury.gov.uk/walker_review_information.htm> (accessed 7 December 2012).

[14] FRC, 'Comply or Explain: 20th Anniversary of the UK Corporate Governance Code' <http://www.frc.org.uk/getattachment/823aa805-72a6-471f-a9be-ccade4737995/Comply-or-Explain-20th-Anniversary-of-the-UK-Corporate-Governance-Code.aspx> (accessed 7 December 2012).

clearly that the debate about corporate governance continues. As we have seen, this is entirely in accordance with the view of the Committee that the Code represented best practice to which companies should aspire, rather than a fixed minimum standard, and should be kept under review in the future. A major contribution of the Committee lay in the introduction of the corporate governance conversation, both within boards and between boards and their investors and others with interests in their companies.

Codes

The balance between voluntary codes and statutory requirements continues to figure in the debate. Although some commentators considered the Code to be an attempt to stave off regulation, the Committee viewed legislation and self-regulation, with the aim of implementing best practice, as complementary. However, statutory measures were liable to reduce compliance to a minimum standard rather than assisting boards to consider the arrangements most appropriate for their company in the light of the spirit of the Code, which aspired to instil best practice and raise standards in that way. There is little doubt that codes of best practice, however they are embedded into regulatory regimes, have an important role to play in establishing standards of corporate governance, and the Cadbury Committee pioneered this widespread acceptance.

A developing stream of academic research analyses the impact of code adoption worldwide. In a widely cited article, Aguilera and Cuervo-Cazurra (2004) placed the Cadbury Code in its historical context by mapping the evolution of corporate governance codes throughout the world. They provided a detailed analysis of the influences on code adoption in the context of varying institutional arrangements. In analysing the drivers of code innovation, they emphasized the need to classify codes according to the issuing body, and they identified six such types: stock exchanges, governments, directors' associations, managers' associations, professional associations, and investors' associations. Their categorization (2004: 425) demonstrated that issuer types have varied over time but, where a code has been developed by a stock exchange in collaboration with other organizations, they deemed the stock exchange to be the issuing body, placing the Cadbury Code in this category. Our study indicates that this gives undue weight to only one of the influences on the process that resulted in the Cadbury Code, and the significant role of the accountancy profession in this suggests that some qualification is needed of their observation that: 'in no country did a professional association develop the first code' (2004: 423–4).

Cicon et al. (2012) also considered issuer identity in examining the thematic content of codes of EU countries. They identified issuers as: government, stock exchange, trade/industrial associations, and composite (issuer including members from at least two of the preceding groups—that is, 'a hybrid of interests and perspectives'). They classified the UK Code, as adopted in 2000, as government issued, on the basis presumably that the FRC is a national regulatory authority. They used this classification in analysing the thematic content of the codes, noting that codes issued by stock exchange and government emphasize accounting and disclosure. They argued that issuer identity is important for understanding code design and in establishing the primary theme.

In understanding the drivers of code adoption, it is important to recognize the political influences, the complex network of relationships among interested groups, and the role of key individuals. The work of Jones and Pollitt (2002, 2004) offered valuable insights into the influences on developments in the UK. As the story of the Cadbury Committee demonstrates, the construction of recommendations by committees is a process that usually depends on a series of hidden compromises. The individual positions of those involved in the process and the ideology inherent in the institutional context in which they are working underpin the development of the regulatory framework. As Maclean, Harvey, and Press (2006: 4–5) noted, 'changes to corporate governance practices introduced in the wake of key governance reports are only ever likely to be stable if matched by parallel changes in assumptions, values and beliefs at the ideological level'. The Committee's original intention was that explanation should play a key role in raising corporate governance standards, but in the initial adoption of the Code the focus of investors appeared to be on a narrow view of compliance: it has taken two decades for the spotlight to shift decisively towards the improvement of explanations.

Consensus

Macdonald and Beattie (1993: 304) used the metaphor of a jigsaw to describe the complexity of the system of corporate governance, which, being 'a mixture of law, self-regulation and best practice', had developed in an unstructured way. Reforms had not considered the system as a whole, and they argued that a major contribution made by the Cadbury Committee had been to consider the issues involved in a coordinated way and to institute a programme of ongoing monitoring and review. This coordination, which involved recognizing and working with other concerned groups, taking account of their work while maintaining the boundaries of the Committee's remit, underpinned the consensus that the Committee had always realized would be fundamental to the Code's success.

Consensus within the Committee was important. Cadbury took considerable care in discussing the drafts that he and Peace produced with Committee members, both inside and outside the meetings, and in checking back regularly with the Committee's sponsors. In December 1991, for example, he wrote to Hugh Smith, Dearing, and Lickiss: 'I would like to be quite sure that

I have a clear view about why our sponsors set us up and what they want us to address.'[15]

One Committee member observed:

it was a fantastic educational process...by the end of it I really did understand something about corporate governance, and I could see that it was an area that needed attention in its own right. I think we all began to be much clearer about...the fact that we were doing something that was rather new. And because...everybody approached this from different perspectives, this was genuinely a case where a group of people came together and developed something which was different from what each of them separately might have done.

Maybe I've just got a sort of golden glow over the whole thing, but...I can think of bodies and meetings which I've been in where there have been huge problems, you know, dysfunctional arguments...nothing that comes to mind on this one, it seems to me on the whole the thing was done very, very smoothly and that's partly because...there was a sort of increasing *esprit de corps* and desire to get the thing done and done well, because...we all began to see that actually it was quite important—not just another committee.[16]

Other interviewees commented on the difference between the Cadbury Committee and others they had sat on:

it was a friendly and informal working party—much less formal than any that I've been on.[17]

---

[15] CAD 01135.
[16] Interviewee L.
[17] Interviewee S.

Normally an ordinary committee isn't the way in which you develop a set of proposals which have never existed before, which are, in a sense, missionary where you need to communicate them and persuade people.[18]

In the early days comments on both the membership of the Committee and its remit were very carefully considered, reflecting the understanding that the successful adoption of the Committee's ultimate recommendations would rest squarely on consensus as to the legitimacy of the Committee and the knowledge and expertise of its members. The response to the draft Report was fully discussed, and the amendments made, while seeming at one level relatively minor, reflected considerable thought by members:

How was the draft report received? I think we were all surprised. We thought... I thought it was rather good, and it got on the whole pretty badly received as I recall. You know you got a lot of flak. And that was quite sobering because we felt we'd done actually quite a good job in terms of the balance there. And suddenly to find these people attacking us for all sorts of things that we didn't realise were problems... undermining the basis of the financial system... the end of the sort of market system as we know it... undue interference and the rest—my recollection is most of it was anxiety about over interference, not the other way round. I can't remember that we had very many people saying it's not going far enough. Because by that time of course the scandals had sort of died down, the recession taken its toll and there were less people going bust because they were

<hr />

[18] Interviewee M.

going bust, rather than because there were some problems on corporate governance. And so we did look carefully at it.[19]

As this comment indicates, a changing external environment had much to do with the responses.

You know sometimes you'd get lucky, and there was unquestionably a mood for change by the time we produced our report. I don't think there was the same mood for change when we started—I think we felt we might have a big job to convince people. Maxwell's demise was absolutely central in changing moods.[20]

Even while the Committee was deliberating, changes in the external environment, some of which we noted in Chapter 1, were accelerating, with dimensions that ran much more deeply and more widely than the Maxwell affair. A DTI-sponsored review of UK company law in the mid-1990s suggested some of the difficulties facing both the Cadbury Committee and its successors:

Recent changes in the organisation of work, production, governance and culture have rendered the ideal of a unitary company law even more problematic. Variously termed, 'post-Fordism', 'post-modernism', the 'risk society' and the 'network society', these contradictory tendencies include the shift to more flexible, decentralised forms of labour processes and work organisation associated with greater work and production flexibility, the rise of the new 'information technologies' which increasingly supply much of the framework of society, of

---

[19] Interviewee L.
[20] Interviewee M.

increasingly fragmented and specialised markets, the 'hollowing out' of the state, the growth of a world market combined with the increasing scale of industrial, banking and commercial enterprises, the emergence of globalised economies whose substance consists of endlessly complex financial flows, and the gradual metamorphosis of industrial corporations from hierarchies of established offices to networks that sit uncomfortably with territorially based forms of organisation, such as the nation state. (Sugarman 1997: 230)

Designing Policy and Regulation by Committee

Our study of the papers in the archive has raised several questions pertinent to policy-making committees and their work, many aspects of which remain opaque. Firstly, what is the relationship between the committee and the sponsoring body (or bodies) and who decides on the remit of the committee? Where there is an institutional 'umbrella', the relationship with sponsors may be straightforward, but we have seen that Cadbury thought it important to spend considerable time ensuring that the Committee's thinking would enable the expectations of the sponsors to be met. This was less problematic in the case of the FRC and the Stock Exchange, since Dearing and Hugh Smith (as members) provided strong support from the start, but, even so, this support was not taken for granted. In his speech to PIRC in November 1991, Cadbury expressed some caution on this: 'We do have a real opportunity to make an authoritative statement of best practice if the bodies represented on the Committee swing behind it.'[21]

However, the accountancy profession, while united in concern over the issues addressed by the Committee, was far from united in its view of the action to be taken to address them. The critical responses to the draft Report from major firms like Arthur Andersen and Ernst & Young demonstrate this very clearly, and expectations of a more radical approach were shared by individual respondents from the profession. D. J. Hughes, who described himself as a chartered accountant working in British industry, wrote: 'I am afraid the draft report is far too British. It is genteel and gradualist and lacks any radical proposals to deal with the crisis and seems a lost opportunity to help our capital markets move into the twenty-first century.'[22]

Changing influences within sponsoring bodies may also have an impact. As we have seen in Chapter 5, the Stock Exchange perspective shifted when Kemp Welch took over as chair from Hugh Smith and Lawrence became chief executive. In 1994 Lawrence was invited to deliver the prestigious Coopers & Lybrand Lecture at the University of Wales, Aberystwyth. He clearly saw a greater role for the Stock Exchange in enforcing corporate governance requirements, dismissing the idea of legislation and observing in passing: 'To leave it to committees to produce guidelines on accountability when those

---

[21] CAD 01166.
[22] CAD 02219.

committees have little accountability or natural authority seems a curious way of proceeding!' (Lawrence 1994: 11).

The Committee's remit appears to have evolved through negotiation with the sponsoring bodies over a period of time. Definition of boundaries was no easy task, as the work of the other groups addressing the issues needed to be taken into account. As Cadbury observed in his speech to PIRC:

> The Committee on the Financial Aspects of Corporate Governance is not a title which lends itself to a snappy acronym. It does not have much of a PR ring about it and 'financial aspects' tended, when we were first formed, to be dropped off which led to misunderstandings.[23]

These misunderstandings persisted and underpinned much of the subsequent criticism of the Committee's recommendations. In the same speech he made it very clear that 'the remit is not to redesign boards; it is to recommend ways of improving standards of financial information and systems of financial control'. However, the death of Robert Maxwell and the revelations about his business activities that followed presented a further challenge, as expectations were raised that the Committee would present solutions to the problem of the dominant chairman. While this event prompted the Committee to review its thinking on broader areas of board responsibility, the focus of the remit remained unduly narrow, according to some commentators on the draft Report. In

---

[23] CAD 01166.

the view of the accountancy firm Arthur Andersen, for example:

it is disappointing that the Report does not discuss the advantages and disadvantages of alternative forms of governance and encourage experimentation. In particular its acceptance without discussion and debate that the unitary board can realistically fulfil the roles of supervision, control and management in all circumstances is open to challenge.[24]

A second set of questions relates to the composition of the committee. How are the members appointed? Are members representative of specific groups or appointed for their particular knowledge and expertise?

Decisions by the sponsoring bodies about the recruitment of Committee members remain a mystery. The chairman had no involvement in this and, as we have seen, was immediately faced with criticism as to the representation of company interests. The appointment of Hogg as adviser was intended to alleviate some of these concerns. Such criticism was taken very seriously, as, in spite of the commitment of the sponsoring bodies, Cadbury was aware from the start that the composition of the Committee would be crucial to views on the legitimacy of its conclusions.

As we have seen, some Committee members saw themselves as representative of specific organizations—for example, de Trafford and the IoD—while others saw themselves as independent, in spite of close connections with

---

[24] CAD 02361.

interested bodies—Charkham, for instance, distanced himself from his links with the Bank of England. Where committee members are viewed—and view themselves—as representative, a further question arises as to how they manage consultation with the bodies they represent to ensure that such representation is effective.

Whether fulfilling a representative role or not, committee members inevitably bring their own individual perspectives to the committee table, and resolving the tensions that these varying positions may present is a challenge for the chairman. Balancing the dynamics of a committee to ensure that all members have an equal opportunity to voice their views is no easy task, and the individual meetings that Cadbury held with members enabled him to undertake the tricky process of integration. One Committee member categorized the members for us as either 'missionaries' or a 'safe pairs of hands' on the basis of his perception of their contributions. The inevitable compromises on the route to consensus usually remain hidden from view, but the Cadbury papers provide a unique insight into how the process was managed, a process that extended well beyond formal meetings. So a third set of pertinent questions relating to how policy-making and regulatory committees work focuses on how the work of the committee is managed, in terms of formality of process, the pattern of consultation, information gathering and processing, and discussion. Are the consultations genuine or simply legitimizing processes? What difference does the publication of the consultation responses on websites make?[25] Such committees gather extensive amounts of information through consultation processes: how do they assimilate this and how does it influence their deliberations? How is the output produced?

We have been able to trace some of these processes for the Cadbury Committee: the summaries of meetings with individuals and of consultation responses, together with the discussion papers produced for the formal meetings, give some indication of how the Committee's thinking evolved in the development of the Code and recommendations. In exploring the continuing work of the Committee in the period after the publication of its Report, a unique feature among groups charged with the development of the UK corporate governance regime, we have also been afforded an unusual insight into how such a committee might influence the adoption of its conclusions.

Our account of the Cadbury Committee demonstrates that each of these three sets of questions needs to be considered if the committee is to be seen as credible and legitimate, which will influence whether its recommendations are adopted.

Managing Expectations

Freeman, Pearson, and Taylor (2012: 6) have recently commented: 'It is remarkable how many of those advocating

[25] For future researchers the question of how long such data will remain available and whether hard copies are retained could be important.

remedies for corporate governance problems today appear to be entirely unaware of the fact that similar problems, with similar remedies proposed, have been recurring in business for centuries.' In contrast to this assertion, Cadbury was only too aware of the persistence of such problems through history and the challenge of attempting to resolve any of them, as his quoting from a speech from the ICAEW president in 1934 shows.[26] At that time too there had been incidents of corporate collapse, followed by calls for clarification of the responsibilities of company directors and auditors, as well as criticism of the passivity of shareholders. However, he went on to argue that there was a greater possibility for improvement this time round:

We are looking to capture the tide of corporate and city opinion and consolidate best practice as standard practice. A window of change *is* now opening. Doubts about the way in which the present system of financial accountability is operating are combined with a general willingness to look at how it could be improved.

Others had used the same metaphor: Tweedie, the ASB chairman, had expressed serious concern about the damaging loss of trust in the accountancy profession and noted that there was 'just a short window of opportunity' to take action while the economy was in recession.[27]

---

[26] CAD 01166.
[27] CAD 01231.

Hugh Collum, in the context of the need to reduce diversity in international accounting standards, had also referred to a 'window of opportunity' for the Committee.[28]

But Cadbury was also keenly aware that the Committee had begun work in a climate of unrealistic expectations: 'Partly because the remit was thought to be wider than it is, expectations as to what we might be able to achieve were exaggerated at the outset.'[29]

Committee members were well aware that there would be criticism of the draft Report: as noted in Chapter 3, the use of the word 'vulnerability' in the preparation for the launch demonstrates this.[30] Throughout the Committee's life and particularly in the period following the publication of the Report, the chairman and members worked hard to address the gap between expectations and what they had been able to achieve. A close eye was kept on reports and comment in the media, as well as in academic and professional journals, and on several occasions steps were taken to pursue the publication of a correction to misunderstandings or a rebuttal to criticism.[31]

The history of regulatory developments can become compressed and oversimplified. With hindsight, cause

[28] See Chapter 3; CAD 01243.
[29] CAD 01166.
[30] CAD 01293.
[31] See Chapter 5 for more detail. Early issues of *Corporate Governance: An International Review*, edited by Bob Tricker, provided an important arena for debate: see, e.g., Arthur (1993) and Cadbury (1993).

and effect can appear amenable to convenient summary.[32] The simplification of cause and effect becomes 'the conventional wisdom'[33] and the evidence that might support any challenge to this widely accepted set of ideas may vanish. It is important to place the Cadbury Committee in the framework of concerns about corporate behaviour that had developed in the decades before its establishment, rather than to characterize it as simply a reaction to the corporate scandals of the 1980s. These may be more accurately viewed as catalysts, prompting action by several groups of interested parties, at a specific time when a 'window of opportunity' had opened.

On 30 June 1995, Lipworth wrote to Cadbury:

> Today marks the formal end of the Cadbury Committee and I should like to take the opportunity to congratulate you on a most remarkable and outstanding achievement.
>
> ...the pioneering work of the Committee has had, and will continue to have a profound influence on the UK's business culture and climate. It could not have started life under less auspicious circumstances, with public confidence in business

---

[32] The assumption that the failure of Enron led directly to the Sarbanes–Oxley Act in the USA is a recent example: a more detailed analysis of events suggests that the ideas behind the legislation may have pre-dated the company's collapse in the minds of politicians and regulators. 'What is perhaps most striking in the legislative process is how successful policy entrepreneurs were in opportunistically coupling their corporate governance proposals to Enron's collapse, offering as ostensible remedies for future "Enrons," reforms that had minimal or absolutely no relation to the source of that firm's demise' (Romano 2005: 1526).

[33] The term popularized by John Kenneth Galbraith in his 1958 book *The Affluent Society*.

and professional standards at a particularly low point. That investors' confidence has been restored is very largely attributable to your work and to the Code and Report.

Not only have overall standards been raised significantly, but there is general acceptance and awareness of the need for proper controls and the importance of curbing excessive power in company chairmen or other directors, as well as the benefits of strong and independent non-executive directors. You broke new ground and the detailed and careful analysis and clear thinking you brought to bear in what were otherwise rather woolly areas will have a beneficial effect for years to come.[34]

Our story of the Cadbury Committee ends here. The Code of Best Practice formed the basis for the current UK Corporate Governance Code, held under the 'umbrella' of the Financial Reporting Council. The Code is regularly reviewed, in recognition of the need to adapt its requirements to the changing corporate landscape. Reviews rely on a process of wide consultation, to maintain the consensus that the Committee originally established. Many of the challenges of corporate accountability and control that the Committee attempted to address remain the subject of the continuing corporate governance conversation, albeit in a very different and rapidly changing corporate world.

---

[34] Unnumbered paper.

Appendix 1

Members of the Committee

Adrian Cadbury

George Adrian Hayhurst Cadbury CBE (born 1929) was educated at Eton and Kings College, Cambridge. In 1952 he joined the firm of Cadbury Brothers Ltd, established by his family in the nineteenth century, becoming its chairman in 1956. After the merger of Cadbury and Schweppes, he served as deputy chairman from 1969 and succeeded Lord Watkinson as chairman of the combined company at the end of 1974; he retired as Chairman in 1989. He received a knighthood for services to the industry in 1977.

Sir Adrian also served as a director of IBM UK Ltd between 1975 and 1995. Between 1990 and 1994 he was a member of the UK Takeover Panel. He chaired the CBI's Economic and Financial Policy Committee between 1974 and 1980 and PRO NED between 1984 and 1995. He was a director of the Bank of England from 1970 to 1994.

Ian Butler

Ian Geoffrey Butler CBE (born 1925) served as chairman of the CBI's Companies Committee. A chartered accountant by trade, he served on a number of boards. He was a director of Barclays PLC from 1985 to 1988, and was on the board of the Cookson Group PLC from 1992 to 1997, serving for some time as chairman.

Jim Butler

(Percy) James Butler CBE (born 1929) was educated at Marlborough and graduated with a degree in mathematics from Clare College, Cambridge. After national service between 1947 and 1949, he joined KPMG (then Peat Marwick Mitchell & Co.) as an articled clerk in 1952, progressing to partner in 1957, managing partner in 1980–5, and senior partner from 1986 to 1993. He served on the executive committee and council of KPMG from 1987 to 1993, was a member of the European Board of KPMG from 1989 to 1993, before becoming chairman of KPMG International in 1991. He retired from the firm as senior partner in 1993. Subsequently he held various directorships, including Camelot, Save the Children, the Royal Opera House, Eurostar, and Wadworth and Co. Ltd. He received a knighthood in 1981.

Jonathan Charkham

Jonathan Philip Charkham (1930–2006) was the grandson of Russian refugees and was educated at St Pauls and Jesus

College, Cambridge. His career spanned law, manufacturing, the Civil Service, and the Bank of England, and he held a number of directorships. He was called to the Bar in 1953, and then worked in the family business (bed and pillow manufacturers) before and after it was taken over by Rest Assured. He joined the Civil Service in 1969, becoming an under-secretary and ultimately heading the Whitehall Public Appointments Unit. He was seconded to the Bank of England, where he became chief adviser to the governors. It was here he was involved in setting up PRO NED in the wake of the UK's secondary banking crisis. He was PRO NED's first director in the period 1981–5. He left the Bank of England after the Cadbury Report, and was subsequently a director of Great Universal Stores until 2001, and took on teaching and advisory work for the World Bank, OECD, and authored books on corporate governance. He was appointed a Sheriff of the City of London in 1994.

Hugh Collum

Hugh Robert Collum CBE (1940–2004) was educated at Eton before qualifying as an accountant at Coopers & Lybrand in 1964. Collum joined Plymouth Breweries, becoming a director of the regional brewer, with which his family had a long connection. It formed a defensive alliance with Courage, being finally absorbed by the Courage group in 1971. In 1973 he became financial director of Courage's then parent company, Imperial Group, until 1981, when he moved to a similar role at Cadbury Schweppes. Collum joined the Beechams pharmaceuticals group in 1987, and, when it merged with Smith Kline, he became chief financial officer until it merged again with Glaxo Wellcome in 2000. He became chairman of British Nuclear

Fuels in 1999, leading the company through partial privatization before his retirement in 2004. He received a knighthood in 2004.

Dermot de Trafford

Dermot Humphrey de Trafford CBE (1925–2010) was educated at Harrow and graduated from SOAS at the University of London in 1943. He served in the Navy from 1943 until the end of the war. De Trafford returned to complete his education at Christ Church College, Oxford, where he read Philosophy, Politics, and Economics. Upon graduation he became a management accountant, with positions at Clubley Armstrong and Orr and Boss. During the 1950s he served on the board of several industrial firms that merged together to form the General Hydraulic Power Group in 1961; of that he became its first managing director and, in 1966, its chairman. In 1976 GHP merged with Low and Bonar, and, following a time as vice chairman, he was appointed chairman in 1982. He became a director of Imperial Continental Gas Association in 1963, serving as deputy chairman from 1972 to 1987; within this role he also chaired a number of their UK subsidiaries, including Calor Gas and Compair. During this period he also served as a director of Petrofina SA. He retired from business in 1990. De Trafford also had a career in banking, serving on the board of several European Financial Institutions, including BNP Paribas, Banque Belge Ltd, and Belgian and General Investments. He served as chairman of the Institute of Directors between 1990 and 1992 and vice president between 1993 and 1994.

Ronald Dearing

Ronald Ernest (Baron) Dearing CBE (1930–2009) was born in Hull, the eldest son of a dock's clerk, and educated at the Malet Lambert Grammar School, Hull. He joined the Civil Service in 1946 as a clerical officer, and, while at the Ministry of Power, he studied for and gained a BSc in Economics in 1954. By 1967, as assistant secretary, he was one of two deputy heads of the coal division at the Ministry of Power. He served in various ministries, including the DTI in 1965–83, becoming under-secretary and then deputy secretary. He was chairman of the Post Office in 1981–7 and chairman of the CNNA in 1987–8. He served on the Accounting Standards Review Committee in 1987–8 and was chairman of the Financial Reporting Council in 1990–3. In 1998 he was made a life peer. He authored a landmark review of higher education in 1997, which had significant implications for improving access to and the quality of higher education and the subsequent introduction of tuition fees.

Christopher Hogg

Christopher Hogg CBE (born 1936) was educated at Marlborough, followed by Oxford University and Harvard. As a young man he saw active service with the Parachute Regiment in Cyprus and Suez. Before his career in industry he worked for three years in corporate finance in the City and for two years in the public sector. He began his career in industry with Courtaulds in 1968, becoming a director in 1973, and chair and chief executive in 1980–91. He was a non-executive director and subsequently chairman of Reuters Group, SmithKline

Beecham, and then GlaxoSmithKline and Allied Domecq. He has also been a member of the UK Department of Industry's Industrial Development Advisory Board from 1976 to 1980, a non-executive director at the Bank of England from 1992 to 1996, and was chairman of the Financial Reporting Council from 2006 until 2010. He received a knighthood in 1985.

Andrew Hugh Smith

Andrew Colin Hugh Smith CBE (1931–2012) came from an influential and prolific financial dynasty. One of his ancestors, Thomas Smith, founded a bank in Nottingham in the 1650s that ultimately became part of NatWest. Hugh Smith was educated at Ampleforth, served with the Royal Horse Guards in Germany in 1950 for his National Service, before returning to Trinity College, Cambridge, to read History and Law. He was then called to the Bar in Inner Temple, where he practised for four years. However, he came to stockbroking after experience with textile conglomerate Courtaulds, which he had joined in 1960. Following success at the Gossard lingerie subsidiary, Hugh Smith was headhunted into the stockbroking firm of Capel-Cure Carden in 1968, becoming a partner two years later and playing a crucial role in its transformation after the market crash of the 1970s to form Capel-Cure Myers. He became a senior partner in his own firm, Capel-Cure Myers, in 1979, a firm that he expanded against the backdrop of the Big Bang reforms of 1986 before finally negotiating its sale to Grindlays, which subsequently was subsumed by the Australia and New Zealand Bank Group. The broking business was then merged into ANZ Merchant Bank, with Hugh Smith becoming deputy chairman.

He joined the council of the Stock Exchange in 1980 and was its chairman from 1988, a period of great change. Hugh Smith oversaw the replacement of the Exchange's council with a new board structure. In 1993, in the light of the scrapped Taurus settlements project, he temporarily took over the role of chief executive. He retired from the chair in 1994. In his later years he served as chairman of the gunmakers Holland & Holland, and on the European advisory board of Accenture. He received a knighthood in 1992.

Andrew Likierman

(John) Andrew Likierman CBE (born in 1943) has had a career spanning the public and private sectors, through both his academic and his professional life. Educated at the University of Vienna and Balliol College, Oxford, he began his career as a management accountant at Tootal Limited from 1965 to 1968. He began lecturing at the University of Leeds Department of Management in 1968, staying there until 1974. During this period he also served as managing director of the overseas division of Qualitex Ltd. He then started and ultimately sold his own business selling business books. He joined London Business School (LBS) in 1974–6, rejoining in 1979. He became director of the Institute of Public Sector Management in the period 1983–8, earned a chair in Accounting and Financial Control in 1987, and progressed to the position of Dean of the LBS in 2009.

Likierman's public-sector career encompassed a number of leadership and advisory posts within the Cabinet Office; he spent a ten-year period as one of the managing directors of the

UK Treasury and Head of the UK Government Accountancy Service (1993–2004). He was a non-executive director of the Bank of England in 2004–8, before resigning to become the chair of the National Audit Office. At present he holds a non-executive directorship at Barclays Bank PLC. He is a past president of CIMA and was for several years a member of the Financial Reporting Council. He received a knighthood in 2001.

Nigel Macdonald

Nigel Colin Lock Macdonald (born 1945) started his career as an articled clerk at Thomson McLintock from 1962 to 1968. He subsequently spent twenty-seven years at Ernst & Young as a partner and senior partner between 1976 and 2003. During this period he served as vice chairman of the Accounting and Audit Committees of Ernst & Young's worldwide practice. Macdonald joined the board of James Lock and Co. Ltd as a non-executive director in 1979, becoming chairman in 1979. He is a member of the Institute of Chartered Accountants of Scotland, serving as its president between 1993 and 1994. Between 1994 and 2001 he was a member of the Industrial Development Advisory Board of the UK Government, and from 1992 to 2004 he was a member of the British Standards Institution and chairman of its Audit Committee. He was a member of the Review Panel of the Financial Reporting Council from 1990 to 2006, and from 1999 to 2005 he was a member of the UK Competition Commission, serving on its specialist panels on electricity and water.

Mike Sandland

Eric Michael Sandland (born 1938) served as a director of the Norwich Union Insurance Company (now Aviva) and was closely involved with the ABI and ISC.

Mark Sheldon

Mark Sheldon CBE (born 1931) served with the Royal Signals as part of his National Service, between 1949 and 1950, and then with the Territorial Army between 1950 and 1953. He was admitted as a solicitor at Linklaters & Paines in 1957 following articles between 1953 and 1956. He was a partner between 1959 and 1993; during this period he spent time as resident partner in New York in 1972–4, as senior partner in 1988–91, and joint senior partner in 1991–3. He was chairman of PPP Foundation between 1999 and 2001; he also served as a non-executive director of Coutts and Co. in the period 1996–8. Sheldon joined the Law Society Council in 1978 as one of its specialist members representing company law, serving as the Society's treasurer from 1981 to 1986 and president between 1992 and 1993. He was president of the City of London Law Society in 1987–8. Between 1990 and 1998 he served on the Financial Reporting Council. He received the CBE in 1997.

Appendix 2

The Committee's Remit

The earliest draft of the Committee's terms of reference is dated 25 April 1991.

To consider the following issues and to produce a code of recommended practice, which would command widespread support:

- (i) communications between boards, shareholders (including shareholders' committees) and other shareholders;
- (ii) the case for audit committees including their composition and role, with special reference to the audit and auditors and the internal audit;
- (iii) the auditors' responsibilities, including the extent and value of the audit report—the appointment, remuneration, resignation and dismissal of auditors and their relationship with audit committees;
- (iv) the frequency, clarity and nature of corporate reporting;
- (v) the responsibilities of executive and non-executive directors and other layers of management for planning, for reviewing and reporting on performance, and in relation to illegal acts.

No other revised versions of this have survived in the archive, but it is most likely that some approximation of the Committee's terms of reference as published in the draft and final reports and set out below (it was unchanged between them) was agreed either by the end of the year at the meetings in the autumn of 1991 or at the two-day retreat in January

1992. Comparing the two, we see a slight shift in focus. 'Good practice' replaces 'would command widespread report', the order is changed, the wording becomes more specific, and the reference to 'illegal acts' is removed.

To consider the following issues in relation to financial reporting and accountability and to make recommendations on good practice:

(a) the responsibilities of executive and non-executive directors for reviewing and reporting on performance to shareholders and other financially interested parties; and the frequency, clarity and form in which information should be provided;

(b) the case for audit committees of the board, including their composition and role;

(c) the principal responsibilities of auditors and the extent and value of the audit;

(d) the links between shareholders, boards, and auditors;

(e) any other relevant matters.

References

Aguilera, R. V., and Cuervo-Cazurra, A. (2004). 'Codes of Good Governance Worldwide: What is the Trigger?' *Organization Studies*, 25/3: 417–46.

Aguilera, R. V., and Cuervo-Cazurra, A. (2009). 'Codes of Good Governance', *Corporate Governance: An International Review*, 17/3: 376–87.

Allborn, T. L. (1998). *Conceiving Companies*. London: Routledge.

Alexander, Lord (1990). 'Investor Relations: Does the British System Work?', in NAPF, *Creative Tension*. London: NAPF, 1–11.

Arcot, S., Bruno V., and Faure-Grimaud A. (2010). 'Corporate Governance in the UK: Is the Comply or Explain Approach Working?', *International Review of Law and Economics*, 30: 193–201.

Arthur, T. (1993). 'A Comment on Cadbury', *Corporate Governance: An International Review*, 1/2: 94.

Baker, H. K., and Anderson, R. (2010). *Corporate Governance: A Synthesis of Theory, Research, and Practice*. Hoboken, NJ: John Wiley and Sons.

Baxter, W. (1981). 'Accounting Standards: Boon or Curse?', *Accounting and Business Research* (Winter), 3–10.

Beckett, A. (2009). *When the Lights Went Out*. London: Faber and Faber.

Belcher, A. (1995). 'Regulation by the Market: The Case of the Cadbury Code and Compliance Statement', *Journal of Business Law* (July), 321–42.

Belcher, A. (1996). 'The Invention, Innovation and Diffusion of Self-Regulation in Corporate Governance', *Northern Ireland Legal Quarterly*, 47/3: 322–34.

References

Berle, A. A., and Means, G. C. (1991). *The Modern Corporation and Private Property*. First published 1932. New Brunswick, NJ: Transaction Publishers.

Boswell, J., and Peters, J. (1997). *Capitalism in Contention: Business Leaders and Political Economy in Modern Britain*. Cambridge: Cambridge University Press.

Bowden, S. (2002). 'Ownership Responsibilities and Corporate Governance: The Crisis at Rolls Royce 1968–71', *Business History*, 44/3: 31–62.

Cadbury, A. (1992). *Report of the Committee on the Financial Aspects of Corporate Governance*. London: Gee & Co. Ltd.

Cadbury, A. (1993). 'A Rejoinder to a Comment on Cadbury', *Corporate Governance: An International Review*, 1/3: 170.

Cadbury, A. (1998). 'The Future of Governance: The Rules of the Game', Gresham College lecture <http://www.gresham.ac.uk/sites/default/files/12may98adriancadbury.pdf> (accessed 20 December 2012).

Cadbury, A. (2000). 'The Corporate Governance Agenda', *Corporate Governance: An International Review*, 8/1: 7–15.

Cadbury, A. (2002). *Corporate Governance and Chairmanship*. Oxford: Oxford University Press.

Capie, F. (2010). *The Bank of England: 1950s to 1979*. Cambridge: Cambridge University Press.

Cavers, D. (1953). 'The Economic Consequences of Atomic Attack', *Annals of the American Academy of Political and Social Science*, 290: 27–34.

Charkham, J. (1993). 'The Bank and Corporate Governance: Past, Present and Future', *Bank of England Quarterly Bulletin* (August), 388–92.

Charkham, J. (1998). 'Corporate Governance; Overcoded? Has Hampel Meant Progress?' *European Business Journal*, 10/4: 179–83.

Charkham, J., and Simpson, A. (1999). *Fair Shares: The Future of Shareholder Power and Responsibility*. Oxford: Oxford University Press.

Cheffins, B. R. (2000). 'Corporate Governance Reform: Britain as an Exporter', in *Corporate Governance and the Reform of Company Law*. Hume Papers on Public Policy, 8/1. Edinburgh: The David Hume Institute.

Cheffins, B. R. (2001). 'History and the Global Corporate Governance Revolution: The UK Perspective', *Business History*, 43/4: 47–118.

Cheffins, B. R. (2008). *Corporate Ownership and Control*. Oxford: Oxford University Press.

Cheffins, B. R. (2011). 'The History of Corporate Governance'. ECGI Law Working Paper 184/2012 <http://ssrn.com/abstract=1975404> (accessed 20 December 2012).

Collier, P. (1992). *Audit Committees in Large UK Companies*. London: Institute of Chartered Accountants in England and Wales.

Conyon, M. J., and Mallin, C. (1997). 'A Review of Compliance with Cadbury', *Journal of General Management*, 2: 24–37.

Copeman, G. H. (1955). *Leaders of British Industry*. London: Gee & Co.

Corrin, J. (1993). 'A Blatant Slur on Executive Directors' Integrity', *Accountancy* (April), 81.

Cottrell, P. L. (1979). *Industrial Finance 1830–1914*. London: Methuen.

Cicon, J. E., Ferris, S. P., Kammel, A. J., and Noronha, G. (2012). 'European Corporate Governance: A Thematic Analysis of National Codes of Governance', *European Financial Management*, 18/4: 620–48.

Culpepper, P. (2010). *Quiet Politics and Business Power: Corporate Control in Europe and Japan*. Cambridge: Cambridge University Press.

Dahya, J., and McConnell, J. (2007). 'Board Composition, Corporate Performance, and the Cadbury Committee Recommendation', *Journal of Financial and Quantitative Analysis*, 42: 535–64.

Dahya, J., McConnell, J., and Travlos, G. (2002). 'The Cadbury Committee, Corporate Performance, and Top Management Turnover', *Journal of Finance*, 57/1: 461–83.

Dallas, G. (2004). *Governance and Risk: An Analytical Handbook for Investors, Managers, Directors, and Stakeholders*. New York: McGraw-Hill Professional.

Davies, P. (1978). 'The Bullock Report and Employee Participation in Corporate Planning in the UK', *Journal of Competitive Corporate Law & Securities Regulation*, 1: 245–72.

Davis, W. (1970). *Merger Mania*. London: Constable.

Dearing, R. (1988). *The Making of Accounting Standards*. London: Institute of Chartered Accountants in England and Wales.

Dedman, E. (2002). 'The Cadbury Committee Recommendations on Corporate Governance: A Review of Compliance and Performance Impacts', *International Journal of Management Reviews*, 4/4: 335–52.

References

Demb, A., and Neubauer, F. (1992). *The Corporate Board*. New York: Oxford University Press.

Dine, J. (1994). 'The Governance of Governance', *Company Lawyer*, 15/3: 73–9.

Edwards, J. R. (1982). 'The Influence of Company Law on Corporate Reporting Procedures, 1865–1929: An Exemplification', *Business History*, 24/3: 259–79.

Eells, R. (1962). *The Government of Corporations*. New York: Free Press of Glencoe.

Erturk, I., Froud, J., Johal, S., Leaver, A., Shammai, D., and Williams, K. (2008). *Corporate Governance and Impossibilism*. CRESC Working Paper Series, Working Paper No. 48, CRESC, University of Manchester <http://www.cresc.ac.uk/sites/default/files/wp48.pdf> (accessed 20 December 2012).

Eun, C., and Resnick, B. (2007). *International Financial Management*. Boston, MA: McGraw-Hill/Irwin.

Ezzamel, M. (ed.) (2005). *Governance, Directors and Boards*. Cheltenham: Edward Elgar.

Ferguson, N. (2008). *The Ascent of Money*. London: Allen Lane.

Finch, V. (1992). 'Board Performance and Cadbury on Corporate Governance', *Journal of Business Law* (November), 581–95.

Freedman, J. (1993). 'Accountants and Corporate Governance: Filling a Legal Vacuum?', *Political Quarterly*, 64/3: 285–97.

Freeman, M., Pearson, R., and Taylor, J. (2012). *Shareholder Democracies?: Corporate Governance in Britain and Ireland before 1850*. Chicago, IL: University of Chicago Press.

Gower, L. C. B. (1979). *Gower's Principles of Modern Company Law*. 4th edn. London: Stevens.

Greenbury, R. (1995). *Directors' Remuneration*. London: Gee & Co. Ltd.

Guinness, J. (1997). *Requiem for a Family Business*. London: Macmillan.

Hampel, R. (1997). *Committee on Corporate Governance. Preliminary Report*. London: Stock Exchange.

Hampel, R. (1998). *Committee on Corporate Governance. Final Report*. London: Gee & Co. Ltd.

Hennessy, P. (2007). *Having It So Good*. London: Penguin.

Higgs, D. (2003). *Review of the Role and Effectiveness of Non-Executive Directors* <http://www.ecgi.org/codes/documents/higgsreport.pdf> (accessed 20 December 2012).

Johnson, P. (2010). *Making the Market: Victorian Origins of Corporate Capitalism*. Cambridge: Cambridge University Press.

Jones, I., and Pollitt, M. (2002). *Understanding How Issues in Business Ethics Develop*. Basingstoke: Palgrave.

Jones, I., and Pollitt, M. (2004). 'Understanding How Issues in Corporate Governance Develop: Cadbury Report to Higgs Review', *Corporate Governance: An International Review*, 12/2: 162–71.

Jones, M. (2011). *Creative Accounting, Fraud and International Accounting Scandals*. Chichester: John Wiley.

Jones, R., and Marriott, O. (1972). *Anatomy of a Merger*. London: Pan.

Judt, T. (2011). *Ill Fares the Land*. London: Penguin.

Keasey, K., and Wright, M. (eds) (1997). *Corporate Governance: Responsibilities, Risks, and Remuneration*. Chichester: John Wiley.

Kinross, J. (1982). *Fifty Years in the City*. London: John Murray.

Koza, M. P., and Lewin, A. Y. (1999). 'The Coevolution of Network Alliances: A Longitudinal Analysis of an International Professional Service Network', *Organization Science*, 10/5: 638–53.

Kynaston, D. (1995). *The City of London*, i: *A World of its Own 1815–1890*. London: Chatto & Windus.

Kynaston, D. (2002). *The City of London*, iv: *A Club No More 1945–2000*, London: Chatto & Windus.

Larcker, D., and Tayan, B. (2011). *Corporate Governance Matters: A Closer Look at Organizational Choices and their Consequences*. Upper Saddle River, NJ: FT Press.

Lawrence, M. (1994). *Corporate Governance*. Coopers & Lybrand Lecture, University of Wales, Aberystwyth.

Liggio, C. D. (1974). 'The Expectation Gap: The Accountant's Legal Waterloo?', *Journal of Contemporary Business* (Summer), 27–44.

Lipton, M., and Lorsch, J. (1992). 'A Modest Proposal for Improved Corporate Governance', *Business Lawyer*, 48/1: 59–67.

Littlewood, J. (1998). *The Stock Market: 50 Years of Capitalism at Work*. London: Financial Times.

Macdonald, N. (1997). 'Corporate Governance', *Chartered Secretary* (May), 491–4.

Macdonald, N., and Beattie, A. (1993). 'The Corporate Governance Jigsaw', *Accounting and Business Research*, 23/91A: 304–10.

McIntosh, R. (2006). *Challenge to Democracy*. London: Politico's Publishing.

References

Maclean, M., Harvey, C., and Press, J. (2006). *Business Elites and Corporate Governance in France and the UK*. Basingstoke: Palgrave Macmillan.

McNulty, T., Roberts, J., and Stiles, P. (2005). 'Undertaking Governance Reform and Research: Further Reflections on the Higgs Review', *British Journal of Management*, 16: S99–S107.

Marriott, O. (1967). *The Property Boom*. London: Hamish Hamilton.

Matthews, D., Anderson, M., and Edwards, J. R. (1998). *The Priesthood of Industry*. Oxford: Oxford University Press.

Moore, M. (2009). 'Whispering Sweet Nothings', *Journal of Corporate Law Studies*, 9/1: 95–169.

Myddleton, D. (2004). *Unshackling Accountants*. London: Institute of Economic Affairs.

Ocasio, W., and Joseph, J. (2005). 'Cultural Adaptation and Institutional Change: The Evolution of Vocabularies of Corporate Governance, 1972–2003', *Poetics*, 33: 163–78.

Osman, C. (1992). 'Boardroom Accountability: In Search of a Workable Framework', *International Financial Law Review*, 11/7: 24–6.

Owen, G. (2011). *Evolution or Revolution? Changes in Britain's Boards of Directors from 1960 to 2010*. London: Spencer Stuart.

Page, M., and Spira, L. F (2004). *The Turnbull Report, Internal Control and Risk Management: The Developing Role of Internal Audit*. Edinburgh: Institute of Chartered Accountants in Scotland.

Peasnell, K., Pope, P., and Young, S. (2000). 'Accrual Management to Meet Earnings Targets: UK Evidence Pre- and Post-Cadbury', *British Accounting Review*, 32/4: 415–45.

Plender, J., and Wallace, P. (1986). *The Square Mile*. London: Hutchinson Business.

Porter, B. (1993). 'An Empirical Study of the Audit Expectation-Performance Gap', *Accounting and Business Research*, 24: 49–68.

Pye, A., Kaczmarek, S., and Kimino, S. (2012). 'Changing Scenes in and around the Boardroom: UK Corporate Governance in Practice from 1989 to 2010', in T. Clarke and D. Branson (eds), *The Sage Handbook of Corporate Governance*. London: Sage, 255–84.

Raw, C. (1978). *Slater Walker*. London: Coronet Books.

Reader, W. J., and Kynaston, D. (1998). *Phillips and Drew: Professional in the City*. London: Robert Hale.

Reid, M. (1982). *The Secondary Banking Crisis 1973–75.* London: Macmillan.

Reid, M. (1988). *All-Change in the City: The Revolution in Britain's Financial Sector.* London: Macmillan.

Robb, G. (1992). *White-Collar Crime in Modern England: Financial Fraud and Business Morality 1845–1929.* Cambridge: Cambridge University Press.

Roberts, J. (2012). 'Between the Letter and the Spirit: Defensive and Extensive Modes of Compliance with the UK Code of Corporate Governance', in T. Clarke and D. Branson (eds), *The Sage Handbook of Corporate Governance.* London: Sage, 196–216.

Rollings, N. (2007). *British Business in the Formative Years of European Integration: 1945–1973.* Cambridge: Cambridge University Press.

Romano, R. (2005). 'The Sarbanes–Oxley Act and the Making of Quack Corporate Governance', *Yale Law Journal,* 114/7: 1521–1611.

Rutherford, B. (2007). *Financial Reporting in the UK: A History of the Financial Accounting Standards Committee 1969–1990.* Abingdon: Routledge.

Sandbrook, D. (2011). *State of Emergency. The Way We Were: Britain, 1970–1974.* London: Penguin.

Seidl, D., Sanderson, P., and Roberts, J. (2012). 'Applying the "Comply-or-Explain" Principle: Discursive Legitimacy Tactics with Regard to Codes of Corporate Governance', *Journal of Management and Governance,* (forthcoming, published online January 2012).

Slinn, J. (1993). 'Solicitors and Business Regulation: Attitudes to Company Law in the Nineteenth Century', in E. J. Swan (ed.), *The Development of the Law of Financial Services.* London: Cavendish Publishing Ltd, 143–52.

Spira, L. F, and Gowthorpe, C. (2008). *Reporting on Internal Control in the UK and the US: Insights from the Turnbull and Sarbanes–Oxley Consultations.* Edinburgh: Institute of Chartered Accountants in Scotland.

Spira, L. F., and Page, M. (2003). 'Risk Management: The Reinvention of Internal Control and the Changing Role of Internal Audit', *Accounting, Auditing and Accountability Journal,* 16/4: 640–61.

Sugarman, D. (1997). 'Reconceptualising Company Law: Reflections on the Law Commission's Consultation Paper on Shareholder Remedies: Part 1', *Company Lawyer,* 18/8: 226–82.

References

Taylor, J. (2006). *Creating Capitalism: Joint-Stock Enterprise in British Politics and Culture 1800–1870*. Woodbridge: Boydell Press.

Teo, E.-J., and Cobbin, P. (2005). 'A Revisitation of the "Audit Expectations Gap": Judicial and Practitioner Views on the Role of the Auditor in Late-Victorian England', *Accounting History*, 10/2: 35–66.

Tricker, B. (1984). *Corporate Governance: Practices, Procedures, and Powers in British Companies and their Boards of Directors*. Aldershot: Gower.

Tricker, B. (1998). Editorial, *Corporate Governance: An International Review*, 6/1: 2–4.

Tricker, B. (2012). *Corporate Governance: Principles, Policies and Practices*. Oxford: Oxford University Press.

Turley, S. (1992). 'Developments in the Structure of Financial Reporting Regulation in the United Kingdom', *European Accounting Review*, 1/1: 105–22.

Van Frederikslust, R., and Ang, J. (2008). *Corporate Governance and Corporate Finance: A European Perspective*. Abingdon: Routledge.

Watkinson, H. (1973). *The Responsibilities of the Public Company Interim Report*. London: CBI.

Weir, C., and Laing, D. (2000). 'The Performance–Governance Relationship: The Effects of Cadbury Compliance on UK Quoted Companies', *Journal of Management and Governance*, 4: 265–81.

Zeff, S. (ed.) (2009). *Principles before Standards: The ICAEW's 'N Series' of Recommendations on Accounting Principles 1942–1969*. London: Institute of Chartered Accountants in England and Wales.

Zingales, L. (1998). 'Corporate Governance', in P. Newman (ed.), *The New Palgrave Dictionary of Economics and the Law*. New York: Macmillan, i., 497–503.

Index

Index

Index